THE QUANTUM LEAP...

In Speed-To-Market

Third Edition

by

John R. Costanza

John Costanza Institute of Technology, Inc.
Denver, Colorado   USA

THE QUANTUM LEAP...

In Speed-To-Market

Third Edition

THE QUANTUM LEAP. . .

In Speed-To-Market

Third Edition

John R. Costanza
John Costanza Institute of Technology, Inc.

1996

Publisher

John Costanza Institute of Technology, Inc.

Library of Congress Cataloging in Publication Data

John R. Costanza

World-Class Manufacturing

Copyright © 1990, 1994, 1995, 1996 by

John Costanza Institute of Technology, Inc.
6825 South Galena Street
Englewood, Colorado, USA
Telephone: 1-800-457-4548

ISBN# 9628182-1-6

Printed in the United States of America

Publisher: John Costanza Institute of Technology, Inc.

Demand Flow®, FlowPower® and The Next Generation of Manufacturing Systems® are federally registered trademarks of John Costanza Institute of Technology, Inc. Patent No. 5,440,480. Patents Pending.

Introduction

Over the past several years, we have seen a substantial growth in the manufacturing industry in the Far East. This growth has been largely at the expense of the United States and other Western and European countries. The number of new, better-paying, skilled manufacturing positions in the United States has been and is projected to continue decreasing in comparison with the newly created, lower-paying service industry jobs. At the same time, many long-time industry leaders in American manufacturing have become little more than a telephone hook-up and mail drop for manufacturing companies that have moved their manufacturing out of the country. Japan has used manufacturing to create a tremendous wealth, and their banking community now controls or owns the majority of the top ten banks in the world.

Japanese and Korean manufacturing giants, for the most part, owe their success of recent years not to better management, not to cheaper labor, not to a more pro-business form of government, and not to a better financed industry—they owe their success to a superior manufacturing technology.

This book is about a manufacturing business strategy that encompasses a powerful manufacturing, quality and design technology. This book is by a recognized veteran practitioner and educator of this business strategy and technology who has led many international companies in its adoption. This text describes the power, simplicity and superiority of this manufacturing and design technology and how it has succeeded when adopted by dynamic companies as their business strategy. As such, this text is a road map for the survival and rebirth of a competitive manufacturing industry of global *world-class* producers through the balance of this century and on into the 21st.

The Author

J ohn R. Costanza has been a recognized practitioner, author and advisor in the manufacturing industry for more than 24 years. Prior to founding John Costanza Institute of Technology, Inc., Mr. Costanza worked in senior management, manufacturing, design engineering, manufacturing engineering and materials management for such corporations as Hewlett-Packard and Johnson & Johnson. He had the opportunity to study international manufacturing and engineering technologies and observe the results as they are properly implemented around the world. Based upon his international study and implementation success of a mathematically-based flow manufacturing technology, Mr. Costanza expanded the technology to include all elements of the corporate business strategy and he is recognized as the "Father of DFT" as the person that formalized the Demand Flow® Technology and Business Strategy.

Demand Flow® is a registered trademark of John Costanza Institute of Technology, Inc.

Upon his return to the United States, he founded the international manufacturing technology centers known as the Worldwide Flow College, as part of the John Costanza Institute of Technology, Inc. corporation. Those colleges were chartered to teach and implement his Demand Flow Technology to enable American and Western manufacturing corporations to compete on a global basis.

Again in 1994, for the third straight year, the John Costanza Institute of Technology received the prestigious "1" rating for manufacturing education and implementation, having trained over 26,000 students from 2,500 corporations in 45 different countries. He continues to direct DFT implementations throughout the world, in addition to designing and expanding the Demand Flow technology curriculum for the Worldwide Flow Colleges.

Mr. Costanza is the President and Chief Executive Officer of John Costanza Institute of Technology, Inc., which is headquartered in Denver, Colorado, U.S.A., with offices in San Jose, California, U.S.A. and Nice, France. As an internationally renowned author, Mr. Costanza continues to lecture and implement the business strategy and Demand Flow Technology. He is frequently a top management conference speaker and advisor to organizations worldwide.

Acknowledgments

The road to flow manufacturing excellence is becoming heavily traveled. Unfortunately cluttered by the quick fix "factory furniture movers," it does have an increasing number of true *world-class* Demand Flow® divisions and international practitioners. I would like to compliment and thank the hundreds of corporations that are utilizing Demand Flow manufacturing technology. Despite the success of individual divisions, it may be presumptuous to identify any large multidivisional company as a *world-class* corporation. Today, many corporations have adopted the Demand Flow Business Strategy based upon the success and results achieved by their pioneering divisions. I would like to compliment and thank the individual divisions of these leading corporations for their dedication to achieving the elite recognition as a *world-class* manufacturer.

To all those true Demand Flow practitioners—for their participation, patience, honesty, training and trailblazing—I express my sincere appreciation.

To the staff and associates of the Worldwide Flow Colleges and the John Costanza Institute of Technology, Inc., I praise you for your endurance and dedication to technology, quality and customer satisfaction. Above all, I would like to thank my wife, Linda, and my daughter, Melissa, for their understanding and support during the thousands of hours spent traveling the world during the development and update of this text. Without their reinforcement and rescue, this text could not be written.

Table of Contents

Chapter One

Competing in the Global Marketplace

The global marketplace has changed the rules of business. Economic and political events in countries around the world have created powerful competitors and opened new markets. Free Trade Agreements are occuring across the globe at an increasing rate; the North American Free Trade Agreement (NAFTA) has linked the United States, Canada and Mexico into a single market of 360 million consumers spending up to $6 Trillion annually.[1] The global economy's thirst for economic capital is driving the pace of competition increasingly higher. It is no longer a matter of producing the highest quality

---

1 Source: United States Department of Commerce, Trade Office, U.S. Census Bureau

product if it arrives 3 months late; the marketing window has probably closed or diminished and is crowded with alternative products.

Revolutionary asset management, response to actual customer demand and speed-to-market for new products are key elements for success and growth in today's global marketplace. The manufacturer that does not understand, and is unwilling or cannot adapt to today's competitive climate will soon be in trouble, or worse, out of business.

American manufacturing has generally not demonstrated an ability or willingness to change to compete in this challenging global marketplace. Over the past decade, the United States has slipped from its place as a very powerful economic leader with a strong manufacturing base to a docile international competitor in many industrial markets. The U.S. economy is making a transition from a heavy, industrialized economic base to an economy heavily dependent on service-based industries.

At one time, the label "Made in America" represented competitively priced products recognized for quality and durability. Today, while there are a few companies in selected industries making high-quality, competitive products, goods made in America are hard to find and they do not enjoy a monopoly on quality and durability. Offshore manufacturing giants like Sony Corporation, Toyota, Honda and Ricoh are names recognized worldwide in association with high-quality products. The world is changing.

Speed-To-Market and Customer Responsiveness

As the marketplace continues to change and become more competitive, the critical corporate goal will be to take quality products from Design Engineering to the customer as quickly as possible. An objective of this text is to link the technology of flow manufacturing to the techniques of simultaneous engineering to achieve *speed-to-market* and extraordinary customer responsiveness.

Although this objective was important yesterday, it is critical today and will be imperative tomorrow because of the increasingly shorter life cycles of products. Shorter life cycles mean that the first company that produces a product enjoys the highest percentage of profit associated with initial product introduction. As competition enters the market, the opportunity for all companies to make a large profit narrows quickly.

More significantly, as the life cycle shortens, it may cross the period required to recover investment. Companies incurring a long design, prototype, and pre-production process may reach the market too late to recover their investment, not to mention being too late to make any consequential profit (see Figure 1-1).

The shortened product life cycle penalizes companies that do not have a minimal design-through-manufacturing process since they run a greater risk of incurring a loss on each new product introduced. Repeated implementation delays can result in the loss of a product line and risk a corporation's very existence. On the other hand, *speed-to-market* can become a powerful tool that can bring a mediocre manufacturing corpo-

LIFE CYCLE

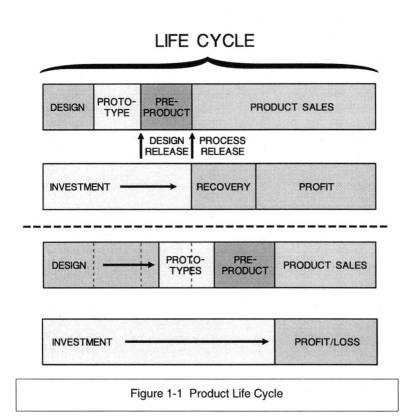

Figure 1-1 Product Life Cycle

ration to a position of market leadership and dominance. With speed-to-market, manufacturers respond to the needs of their customers and adjust appropriately to the rapidly changing forces of the marketplace. Furthermore, when speed-to-market manufacturers run their business at the lowest working capital position possible, they create and enjoy sustained competitive advantage.

Two Different Approaches to Manufacturing and Design

Two radically different manufacturing technologies are developing between various countries and even between corporations within the same country. The first technology, the scheduled production approach, focuses on functional product design and functional manufacturing; this approach and its variations are commonly referred to as Materials Requirements Planning or MRP (also MRP II, ERP). The second technology, Demand Flow® manufacturing techniques, methods and systems, concentrate on process design and focus on material turn-over and minimal overhead support costs.[2]

In analyzing the elements of product cost, the three basic elements are:

1. Material to make the product.

2. Overhead costs for the people and facilities to design, develop and support the product.

3. Direct labor—the employees who typically physically build the product.

Economically, material and overhead elements constitute the largest percentage of product cost. In most discrete manufacturing products, material encompasses the majority of product cost, overhead is the second largest portion of product cost,

---

2   Demand Flow® is a registered trademark of the Jc-I-T Institute of Technology, Inc.

and direct labor contributes the smallest cost factor. A common misconception among U.S. manufacturers is that direct labor constitutes a majority portion of product cost. Thus, manufacturers often focus on the elimination or reduction of direct labor. As a result, some companies consider moving factories to countries where labor costs are lower. These companies are chasing the smallest portion of their product costs while management follows a flawed business strategy.

At Hewlett Packard Company, direct labor typically comprised less than four percent of product cost. Manufacturing in the Western Hemisphere has for years focused on direct labor as a key tool in managing the manufacturing process. Material or components are brought into the manufacturing facility and stored for weeks and months awaiting the availability of scheduled direct labor employees or machines to build the product. Although finished products are not required, material may be brought in early to ensure that production employees are kept busy. This increases the on-hand raw materials and finished goods inventories which, in turn, increase the material and overhead portions of product costs simply to keep production employees busy. Traditional costing and management systems can actually encourage this buildup of inventory levels to create the often misleading impression of labor efficiency and to absorb traditional overhead costs. Often, a product that takes 12 weeks to produce actually has 11 hours of actual work content in it. The solution to rising costs lies in implementing a company-wide business strategy that focuses on material and overhead costs and lowers total costs.

Tracking Skeletons

In the Western world, complex scheduling and tracking systems have been developed to assist management in tracking products through the facility and in tracking the efficiency of direct labor employees within the manufacturing process. Formal computerized systems, such as Material Requirements Planning (MRP) or Manufacturing Resource Planning (MRP II), and Enterprise Requirements Planning (ERP) have been developed to "help" manufacturing planners and buyers determine what to build and which parts to buy based upon manufacturing schedules. Inventory worth millions of dollars is maintained in a manufacturing process that takes weeks or months to create products.

Countries in the Far East, on the other hand, concentrate on developing a high-quality manufacturing flow process that focuses on material and overhead as opposed to the traditional Western approach of focusing on direct labor. This focus is on simultaneous design of the product and flow process at the start of the design cycle, and they have developed techniques to replenish material as it is consumed in the manufacturing process. They pull material as it is required with very simple, yet powerful systems. They make minimal usage of the computer to execute the manufacturing process, utilizing local area networks (LANs) as opposed to the outdated mainframe systems common in scheduled (MRP) manufacturing.

Quality Process Is Essential

The primary focus of the Japanese has been on the development of the relative flow process plus the tools and techniques of taking quality to the employees and machines that create the product. Although they are actively pursuing the mixed-model techniques of Demand Flow® Technology (DFT) that allow them to adjust daily volume and product mix, their initial focus was to produce high-quality products with a minimal amount of overhead and with the lowest possible material costs. Material is pulled into the manufacturing process and fabricated into products which are produced based upon actual customer demand, not upon anticipated market forecasts.

Companies that implement Demand Flow® Business Strategy do not incur the substantial inventory carrying costs borne by the traditional manufacturer who maintains millions of dollars' worth of inventory in on-site warehouse and storage retrieval systems. Because the vast majority of product cost is in material and overhead costs, Demand Flow manufacturers are able to produce products at substantially lower costs, even though their labor costs may rise. In fact, Japanese labor costs have risen to the point where they are higher than those of comparable American industries.

Unfortunately, in the United States and Europe, management and stockholders continue to pressure manufacturers to reduce the direct labor content in a product or to reduce the labor value in a product. Many companies have moved their manufacturing operations offshore in an attempt to reduce the direct labor costs in the product. Simultaneously, they carry millions of dollars of inventory in offshore facilities or in ocean-going vessels that transport the product between the "low-cost" off-shore manufacturing facility and the customer. Uninformed management and politicians can lead companies and countries down the wrong path by continuing to follow outdated business strategies and reporting systems!

A healthy economy will not grow nor create wealth and capital relying upon service-based industries. In the past 15 years, the United States has slipped from the greatest creditor nation in the world to one of the greatest debtor nations in the world.

Japan, on the other hand, has achieved worldwide financial and manufacturing supremacy.

Japan Dominates Employee Productivity Growth

In viewing the world and the competitors' fighting to gain or maintain market share in each of the worldwide manufacturing industries, productivity growth-per-country is a significant factor for the forward-looking company. It is a factor that helps to determine from where the competition is going to come in the years ahead.

While total production output in the United States exceeds that of Japan, this Far East nation has consistently dominated real growth in output-per-employee since the 1970s. Such productivity-growth leadership normally shifts from one nation to another each year, and such has been the case with the runners-up. However, Japan's dominance has been absolute until recently.

A relative newcomer in industrial production power is Korea (see Figure 1-2). Although Japan maintained its rate of growth in output-per-employee and the United States maintained its positive growth rate, Korean growth is nearly double that of Japan. Growth in output-per-employee in Japan is only

GLOBAL COMPETITION
OUTPUT PER WORKER - HOUR IN MANUFACTURING
PERCENTAGE CHANGE

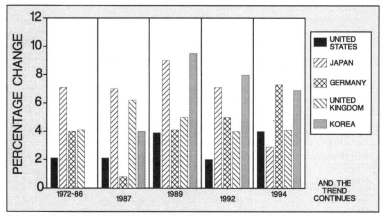

Source: U.S. Department of Labor, Bureau of Labor Statistics, Korean (1994) output est.

Figure 1-2 The Growth of a World-Class Competitor

a part of another major accomplishment: Japan has demonstrated great ability to focus on quality and production costs while they continue to release new products.

We have seen the Korean manufacturing giants attempt to adopt the same technology, tools and techniques as Japan. Perhaps the biggest difference between the two competitive nations is that the Koreans have become known for being more demanding of their employees, but the manufacturing philosophy and many of the flow techniques are exactly the same.

Job Mismatch in the United States

The job market in the United States is marked by mismatches in the nature and availability of jobs and the people to fill them. There are a large number of underemployed people, and there are an increasing number of lower-paid, service-oriented jobs available. It has become harder in many parts of the country to fill those jobs. The number of manufacturing jobs and other higher paid jobs in the United States continues to decrease. The delta in average wage between a created service-based job and a lost manufacturing job is an average of $21,500 per year less for the service job.[3] Manufacturing employment also continues to shrink as a percentage of the United States' job market.

3   Source: United States Department of Labor

The difficulty in filling service-based jobs, whether for a fast-food outlet or a local department store, has prompted some companies to offer such incentives as sign-up bonuses to new employees and finders' bonuses to current employees who bring in qualified job applicants. It has also prompted a more aggressive effort to recruit people for jobs previously filled by placing a help wanted sign in the window.

Low-Paying Jobs Dominate Future

The U.S. Bureau of Statistics' projections promise little change—new jobs will be largely service-oriented and at the low end of the wage scale. The top ten new job categories and the number of new jobs through the year 2000 are projected in Figure 1-3.

In the absence of major modifications in manufacturing practices, top management's commitment to change, and adoption of techniques proven successful in other parts of the global economy, industry in the United States appears to be on a dangerous path. It is a path of creating a great many jobs without the traditional, corresponding creation of appreciable wealth. It is a path of creating jobs which will remain largely unfilled while a portion of the skilled population remains underemployed.

WHERE THE NEW JOBS WILL BE, 1992-2000

Occupation	Number of New Jobs	Percent Change
Retail Sales	1,200,000	33%
Waiter/Waitress	752,000	44%
Nursing	612,000	44%
Janitor	604,000	23%
General Manager	582,000	24%
Cashier	575,000	26%
Truck Driver	525,000	24%
Office Clerk	462,000	20%
Food Counter Worker	449,000	30%
Nursing Aide	433,000	35%

DATA: BUREAU OF LABOR STATISTICS

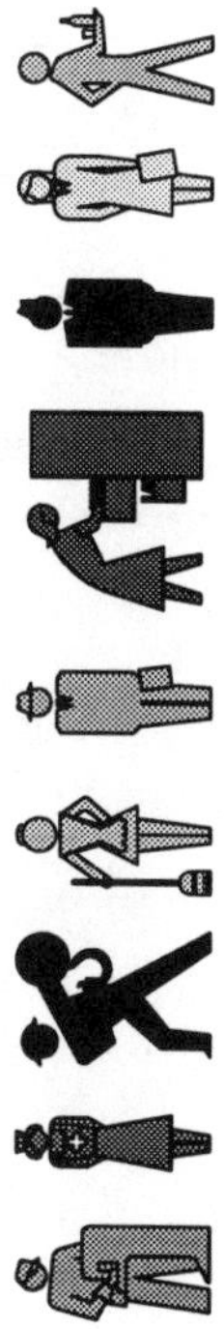

Figure 1-3 New Job Growth

A New Business Strategy for Global Competition

Throughout the 1980s and 1990s, the American dollar was continually devalued against the Japanese yen; during 1994~1995 the dollar was devalued to an all time low against the yen. This created and continues to create an interesting climate for potential problems. When the dollar was devalued 50 percent against the yen, American products became considerably cheaper for the Japanese to buy with their native yen currency. On the other hand, Japanese products bought in the United States with American dollars are considerably more expensive after devaluation. As the dollar has devalued, the Japanese have invested heavily in real estate and other major properties in the United States. Unfortunately, even with the devaluation of the dollar, the trade deficit between the United States and the Japanese did not correspondingly decline.

The Japanese have proceeded to build manufacturing facilities throughout North America and more recently in Europe to take advantage of a relatively cheap labor source which now exists. However, the profit of the product, whether it be manufactured in the United States, Europe, Canada or Japan, is returned to and remains in Japan. A simple analogy to this would be an American consumer who buys products from a Japanese manufacturer. The Japanese manufacturer sells three of its products to the American consumer at $100 per piece. The $300 is moved from the United States to Japan; then through devaluation, the dollar's value drops, relative to the yen. The American consumer can no longer afford to buy the three products, but instead buys only two products for $200 each, which is double the original cost of $100 each. The two products are bought for a total of $400. The consumer paid a total of $100 more for fewer products.

Rather than adopting a strict protectionist policy or allowing continuation of the devaluation of the American dollar, the goals of industry must be to create high-quality products that are competitive in international markets. Global success requires total quality, response to customer requirements, speed-to-market and competitive pricing. Companies cannot acquire these keys with quick fixes and philosophical concepts of employee "quality" and "empowerment" programs while they continue to focus on the elimination or reduction of direct labor and dream in an evolutionary wonderland.

As a competitive business strategy, the revolutionary tools of Demand Flow manufacturing provide an incredible market-driven advantage as companies manage the manufacturing pipeline based upon actual sales rather than anticipated forecasts. Although developed as a boardroom strategy, the exciting power and advantages of Demand Flow manufacturing, speed-to-market and meeting customer demand, quickly spread to all organizations as a companywide business strategy; you need only to talk to a company that has successfully adopted Demand Flow to realize its dramatic enterprisewide impact. Furthermore, Demand Flow is applicable to all manufacturing companies, whether it is a continuous flow, repetitive, made-to-order, assemble-to-order or other manufacturing environment, and regardless of company size.

Having built the manufacturing weapon, the sales organization now gives customers shorter lead times; marketing quickly introduces new products; engineering simultaneously designs new products into the existing flow process; finance takes advantage of cash flow and inventory dollars that have been freed and, most importantly, the mighty customer receives a high-quality product delivered to their request. Recognizable side benefits for the boardroom include a dramatic increase in inventory turns, a radical reduction of finished goods and in-process inventory, increased productivity, reduced manufacturing floor space and lower overhead costs. Costs go down and sustainable competitive power is drastically increased.

To compete successfully in the global marketplace, manufacturing corporations must consider all investments in terms of their ability to fulfill competitive objectives that include product mix, flexibility, response to customer demand and a focus on quality. With Demand Flow manufacturing technology, companies design quality to the flow process and add flexibility required to change from product to product in the shortest period of time and products are built to actual customer demand. The following chapters detail the technique, methods and systems of the Demand Flow Business Strategy.

Chapter Two

Strategy and Technology for World-Class Survival

The prevailing manufacturing process in the United States has been based upon scheduled manufacturing techniques. Typically, products are created based upon a weekly or monthly schedule. Usually, these products are produced in terms of subassemblies or fabricated parts which are scheduled based upon a monthly forecast for the finished products. Lower level assemblies and fabricated parts are included in the final product.

Formalized computer systems have been developed to assist in the traditional scheduling and tracking of these batch subassemblies or machined parts. The formalized computer system designed to schedule subassemblies and/or manufactured parts as well as to buy the required raw materials is commonly referred to as an MRP or MRP II (Manufacturing

Resource Planning; throughout this book "MRP II" will be used to include MRP, MRP II and ERP) computer system. This outdated, elaborate and complex system has been developed over a period of the past two to three decades to assist the scheduled manufacturer. MRP-based systems were developed to assist in the planning, tracking and control of the traditional schedulized manufacturing process. The prevailing manufacturing methodology in the Far East, commonly referred to by the adopting Japanese as Kanban Flow Manufacturing, is often called "pull" or flow manufacturing by Western manufacturers. It would not, however, be correct to call all Far East or Japanese manufacturers flow or *world-class* manufacturers. Although there are a great many truly *world-class* flow manufacturers in Japan, there are also some very conservative and scheduled manufacturers operating in the island nation.

Scheduled versus Flow Manufacturing

The differences between scheduled manufacturing (MRP II) and the technology of Demand Flow manufacturing are substantial, significant and many. There are differences in basic philosophy, strategy, techniques, objectives and utilization of people. The traditional goals of scheduled manufacturing are inventory reduction and reduced lead times. The goals of flow manufacturing are demand driven production with zero in-process inventory and an unparalleled standard of perfection against process capability. Essentially, what may take a scheduled manufacturer several months to produce can be produced by a flow manufacturer in a few hours or days. And, this can be done with greater manufacturing output, substantially higher quality, reduced work-in-process dollars, less work space, reduced scrap and rework materials, increased labor efficiency, and substantially reduced material costs.

Scheduled Production Philosophy

Traditional manufacturing plants are typically designed with functional production departments. They typically have a storeroom for raw materials and subassemblies. Production is accomplished by scheduling a fabricated part or subassembly. These items are then routed from functional department to department based upon a product's or subassembly's scheduled batch or lot quantity. Machinery and assembly areas are arranged by functional work centers or departments. As an example, there may be several similar punch presses grouped together into a single functional press department work center. This functional arrangement could also apply to functional subassembly and test areas (reference Figure 2-1).

In scheduled manufacturing raw material is kept in the storeroom. Once the assembly or fabricated part is scheduled, a work order is released, and the material required to produce the assembly is issued based upon a planned production start date and start quantity. All required material is issued based upon the scheduled quantity of fabricated parts or subassemblies to be produced. After the production item is scheduled and material is issued from the storeroom, the kit or grouping of material is placed into a queue at the workstation or work center where the production is planned to

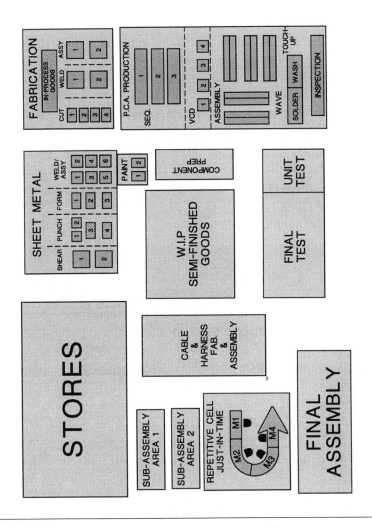

Figure 2-1 Functional Manufacturing Plant

be performed. The scheduling and issuing of material usually takes between a few days and a week. When the scheduled production item has reached the top priority at the work center where the production is to be performed, the kit or group of material is taken out of the work center queue and placed into production. The kit or group of parts is processed from operation to operation until the fabricated part or subassembly is completed. Material usage and labor efficiency are tracked via the work order, and variances are reported when the work order closes.

Quality Exposure of the Lot

Once this scheduled quantity, or lot of parts, is completed, it is traditionally sent to an inspection area for verification of quality. If the parts do not pass inspection, they are returned to the production department for rework. Since all parts were produced in a batch at the same time, the quality-defect exposure level is at the entire lot—*it is very common for the entire lot to be produced with the same defect.* The parts are either reworked, or, if they do pass inspection, they are typically returned to the storeroom either physically or by way of a computer transaction. They can then be processed through the storeroom by another work order that routes the fabricated part or subassembly onto another work center or workstation that will perform the next higher level of subassembly or fabrication. This process will continue until the manufactured item or the subassembly is processed into the top-level product, at which time it becomes available to be shipped to the customer. This multilevel or subassembly manufacturing technology can typically take weeks to produce a product that may contain only a few hours of actual machine or labor content.

Lead Time Inflates Inventory

The number of days that it takes to complete a product from the time that the first, lowest level manufactured item or subassembly is scheduled to start production until the final product is completed is considered to be the manufacturing lead time. There is scheduling and in-process queues, or waiting, at each machine or workstation in production. Subassembly items or kits are often produced in a similar manner: processed functionally, stored, then issued when the final assembly product is scheduled.

These traditional scheduling techniques utilize unnecessary queue or storage of raw materials prior to production. Because of the length of the production process, a large inventory of finished goods is often needed to satisfy a fluctuating customer demand. This traditional manufacturing scheduling process utilizes subassembly manufacturing techniques along with a multilevel bill of material. By its nature of lead times and scheduling, this traditional manufacturing technique requires a substantial amount of inventory in process at all times. Additionally, manufacturers who utilize these scheduling techniques typically realize inventory turnover of ten or less per year. The associated long manufacturing lead times make marketing forecasting difficult since the longer the manufacturing lead time, the more difficult it becomes to predict customer needs further out in time.

Schedulized Manufacturing Kills Customer Responsiveness

The schedulized manufacturing lead time makes it difficult to react quickly to changing customer demand. The lengthy process of long manufacturing lead times, queues at each work-station, and frequent trips to the storeroom place a long period of time between the customer's order and manufacturing's completion of that order. While the manufacturing process is fixed, the customer's position may not be. Indeed, the customer's demand may change before it is satisfied. Customer order acceptance in less than the manufacturing lead time requires manufacturers to carry expensive finished goods inventories.

The longer the manufacturing lead time, the more likely it is that the customer or the marketing forecast may change. Such change would be likely within the traditional manufacturing lead time, and it would require major changes to the actual production plan. While manufacturing personnel will typically complain about the marketing forecast changing, the actual problem lies in the fact that it takes far too long to get a product through the manufacturing process. The longer it takes, the more likely it is there will be a change affecting the scheduled production as marketing strives to be responsive to the customer needs.

Another significant feature of schedulized manufacturing is that if there is no schedule and no issuing of parts, nothing happens in production. Also, the traditional production employee is important to the specific workstation or machine but has little responsibility or authority in the total process and production of units.

Extensive Storage System

Storage and parts handling represent a focal point of batch manufacturing. Raw materials are received, inspected and stored. Then, based upon a schedule, material is issued to the production process. Often such materials are returned to stores in the form of subassemblies or fabricated parts before being issued out again to a higher level subassembly. These nonproductive receiving and storage systems in conventional batch manufacturing often represent a major control and monitor point of the production process as well as being a major contributor to unnecessary overhead costs.

Flow Manufacturing Foundation

Demand Flow Technology is a much simpler but incredibly powerful manufacturing technology. It focuses on a much more aggressive flow process that seeks to eliminate or minimize nonvalue-added work in the production process while emphasizing quality at the machine or production employee level. Its primary objective is to build a high-quality product in the shortest production time and at the lowest possible cost. The

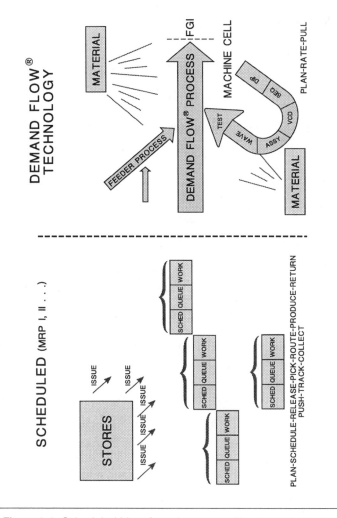

Figure 2-2 Scheduled Manufacturing versus Flow Manufacturing

flow process becomes a sequence of tasks; the product is viewed as a "pile of parts."

A typical flow manufacturing facility may have production lines with feeder lines and/or machine cells feeding into it. There are no distinguishable subassemblies in the production flow process. The process does not result in all milling machines in one location, all drill presses in another, and all trimmers in another, as an example. In flow manufacturing, machine cells consisting of different machines would be arranged with just enough of each to be able to maintain a steady and efficient flow feeding toward the consuming production line. The machine cell is a group of dissimilar machines used to produce a family of similar products.

Products Flow Upon Demand

Where fabrication of an item or assembly is required prior to entering the main line, it is done as a feeder line attached directly to the main line at the point where it is needed. There is minimal external subassembly work, as such, and there is no return of completed work to a place of storage. These feeder lines are flow processes at the point that they are consumed.

The Total Quality Control (TQC) methodology is maintained throughout the production process and is designed and managed to minimize production defects and drive quality into the process. Clear, pictorial TQC method sheet documentation is used to guide employees through the work content and TQC verification process.

Flow manufacturing is based upon a high-quality production process in which products are produced based upon a daily rate. Although this rate and mix can vary each day, it is to be reached every day. Daily fluctuations are in response to actual customer demand. The combined fluctuation can be very significant although it is spread over several days. There is no queuing, no waiting, and no in-process scheduling. Flow manufacturing utilizes a demand pull process. The product is pulled from the back of the process in a flexible and reactive fashion that can reach from product shipping back through the entire production process and can extend to external manufacturing suppliers.

Flexibility and Demand Pull

The Demand Flow manufacturing techniques will work on any product, high- or low-tech, machine- or labor-intensive, once you have met and defeated the resistance that arises from dedicated traditional practitioners. The production process can function well, although at a lower volume, even when almost half of the production team is missing. Demand Flow manufacturing technology is a TOTAL BUSINESS STRATEGY that crosses all organizational boundaries and requires a commitment to revolutionary change from *all* top managers.

The Demand Flow manufacturing methodology is flexible to change, flexible to the planned or unexpected absence of several employees, and flexible to market fluctuations because of its short reaction time. It is far more capable of undergoing major changes in demand in a shorter period of time than is traditional manufacturing.

Flow manufacturing utilizes a demand pull technique to communicate demand-to-build and demand-to-pull material to replace that consumed by already completed products. The demand pull material system utilizes a technique called "KAN-BAN." Kanban is a Japanese word that translates into English as a "communication signal" or "card." Kanban is used to communicate a demand to produce a manufactured item and to literally pull materials to an operation in the process without scheduling. More than a communication card, Kanban is an essential technique in the execution of flow manufacturing. Kanban techniques can be utilized in several different manners, such as a single-card or single-container, a dual-card, or a multiple-card Kanban system. Kanbans and the flexible people who work in flow manufacturing are key elements in allowing the TQC process to be so flexible and responsive.

Process Pull Before Supplier Pull

Initially, the conversion to flow manufacturing will not eliminate the central storeroom. However, that is an ultimate objective. Although the storeroom is an essential part of the traditional schedulized manufacturing philosophy, it is not a required link in the demand pull flow manufacturing philosophy. A major objective of flow manufacturing is to get total inventory turns swiftly to a minimum of 20 per year for competitive survival—and to reach 30 to 60 inventory turns per year soon thereafter.

Initially, the parts will likely be received from suppliers who may have a track record of questionable quality and of not delivering material on time. As the part in question becomes a priority, a flow manufacturer will start working with suppliers to produce higher quality parts that are verifiable in the supplier's process at the supplier's location. Once a quality part has been established, the next priority will be to establish on-time delivery. Freight networks should then be established so that quality parts can be received from suppliers on a more frequent basis without an increase in freight costs. The quality issues must be solved at the supplier and verified at the supplier, and the freight networks must be established. Then the quality materials can be received and taken directly into the flow manufacturing production process without going through an incoming inspection or a storeroom. An area called Raw-In-Process (RIP) inventory will be established. RIP includes a supply area that is very close to the point in the process where the parts are consumed. On an average, RIP will contain approximately one week's worth of raw parts. Over time, the number of parts being delivered from the supplier directly to RIP will increase, and the number of parts being delivered to the central storeroom will decrease.

Focus on Quality, Costs, Turns

The objective of Demand Flow manufacturing is not to take apart the traditional storeroom and scatter the material throughout the production process. The objective is to focus on quality, linear manufacturing, demand pull, and on-time delivery issues to allow the quality parts to be received and taken directly to the production process. Central storerooms are not an essential part of a Demand Flow manufacturing process. Since products are not scheduled and components are not issued to build subassemblies, as in traditional manufacturing, the raw material storeroom is unnecessary in the Demand Flow manufacturing process. Flow manufacturing seeks the highest possible inventory turns and lowest possible overhead. The Demand Flow manufacturer works closely with, but not at the expense of, suppliers to achieve quality parts, on-time delivery, and lower costs.

Total Customer Satisfaction

Many converts to Demand Flow manufacturing are drawn to the overall philosophy because it is market driven. It is guided by and responsive to the changing marketing requirements on a level beyond comprehension of the traditional schedulized philosophy. Since the Demand Flow strategy drastically reduces the manufacturing lead time, marketing will be allowed to make changes in a shorter period of time without impacting the production process. Top management must be committed to an essential element of flow manufacturing—that which requires more frequent input from marketing on a continuing basis. Although changes in the manufacturing daily rate can be made each day, they must be made within a predetermined flexibility agreement negotiated with marketing, manufacturing and the material suppliers.

Horizons Broadened

Demand Flow manufacturing facilitates a more successful marketing effort. The marketing department assists in the production process with both market forecasts and finished goods management. With flow manufacturing, marketing can go after business that could never before be given serious consideration. Flow manufacturing is a companywide total business strategy that starts with the top members of the management team. In addition to the close relationship with marketing, flexibility and absorption of quality control functions, flow manufacturing also gives production a greater impact on, or closer working relationship with, finance, research and development, design engineering and human resources. Many roles change and some departments move from what was their normal functional niche. With Demand Flow Technology, manufacturing becomes your weapon to compete on a global basis.

World-Class Demand Flow Manufacturing

To become a *World-Class* Demand Flow manufacturer capable of competing in a global marketplace, companies need to master these interdependent and crucial elements:

1. Companywide Demand Flow Business Strategy that is driven by top management.

2. Demand-driven manufacturing flow process that is sequenced to customer order activity without production scheduling.

3. Production volume and mix is adjusted each day based upon actual customer demand.

4. Financial management is changed to be consistent with the flow process and labor tracking along with departmental absorption accounting is abandoned.

5. Simultaneous Engineering is practiced to design products and processes concurrently.

6. Total employee involvement is focused to the technical perfection of the product and process sequence of events.

7. Commitment to *A New Way of Life* across all organizational boundaries, not to a project.

The business strategy includes a total commitment from top management for customer-responsive processes based upon a flexible, total quality, flow technology. Customer satisfaction must reign supreme as the corporate goal is to produce the highest quality products with the quickest response to customer and market demands. Although the product has the lowest cost, the selling price for these high-quality products will become a business decision.

The companywide Demand Flow Technology includes TQC, engineering design, linear daily rates, process quality, operational cycle time or Takt time, flexible material forecasting, flow process costing, and backflush management analysis in a Demand Flow manufacturing process. The flexible people involved in flow manufacturing focus on quality and depart from the traditional productivity goals. Production employees enforce quality through the use of operational method sheets, and they are responsible for defined assembly, fabrication, verification and total quality validation. They learn at least two other operations in addition to their primary and can swiftly fill those positions when production volume is adjusted.

Flow manufacturing focuses on people in a different way than does traditional manufacturing. The emphasis on traditional scheduled manufacturing is to cut labor costs, even though labor costs for most efficient manufacturers have dropped to between three and ten percent of product costs. Flow manufacturing focuses on the 90 to 97 percent of product costs—materials and overhead—while emphasizing employee involvement to build a high-quality product using a continually improving process.

Evolution or Revolution

Benefits achieved through the implementation of Demand Flow Business Strategy can provide a corporation with a "Quantum Leap" in the competitive ability to produce high-quality, low-cost and customer-responsive products. Flow manufacturing techniques are fundamentally opposed to many of the techniques of schedulized, departmental, and subassembly production of traditional (MRP II) manufacturing. Progressive corporations desiring to achieve the elite recognition of *world-class* manufacturing must strategically revolutionize their companywide business technology.

Traditional manufacturers who attempt to evolutionarily achieve the flow manufacturing benefits *(MRP II—Lot size of one)* without adopting the fundamental flow manufacturing techniques, methods and systems risk engulfing themselves in a dangerous facade that ultimately will result in minimal competitive benefits. The transition to the flow manufacturing technology is difficult and people naturally resist change, but the benefits are enormous for those with a *leadership commitment and desire to be the best.*

Chapter Three

Flow Technology for World-Class Manufacturing

The key focus of the *world-class* manufacturer is on a customer-responsive, high-quality and extremely efficient flow process. Typically, however, the focus of the traditional Western world manufacturer is not on the production process. Unfortunately, this is the case even though the production process determines the quality of the final product. It is this process which creates items to sell enabling the corporation to maintain profitability. Western world manufacturers must refocus from a strategic viewpoint to the production flow process. As a company becomes a *world-class* flow manufacturer, the way in which the production process is established and the way in which the performance of the process is measured must change significantly. Traditional terms such as manufacturing lead time, work orders, scheduling, queue, reporting, labor tracking, subassemblies, routing, operational efficiency, and others become obsolete.

New Terminology Flow

The new terminology of flow manufacturing has been developed and must be used. The flow manufacturer will become familiar with terms such as TQC, sequence of events, team pass, Kanban, total product cycle time, RIP, linear rates, flexible forecasts, cycle time costing, operational cycle time, Takt time (a German word for rhythm or beat), and many others. Demand Flow Technology is based upon a production flow process that uses Kanbans to pull material into and through the process as the material is consumed. Material is pulled from a nearby point of supply into the rate-based production flow process. It is a flexible pull system that views a product as a "pile of parts" that is pulled through a sequence of events where work is performed by people or machines to create the product.

The underlying objective of DFT is to produce the highest quality product in a customer-responsive flow process.

Building a Demand Flow Process

Demand Flow manufacturing is a pull process, pulled from the back, or the completion, of the product. The pull begins at the very end of the production flow process and continues

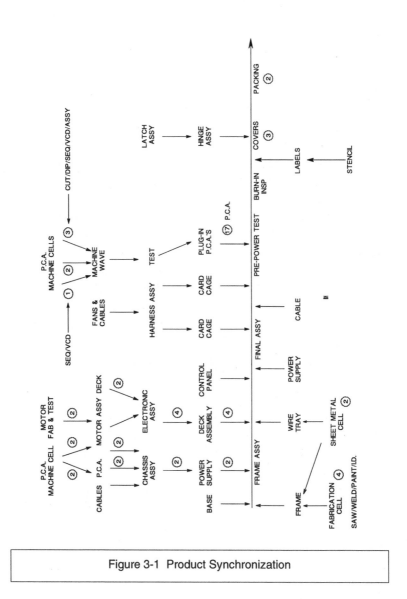

Figure 3-1 Product Synchronization

forward through the flow, through feeder processes and machine cells, to the point-of-usage inventories, and eventually even to suppliers. Parts are pulled into and through the process by a demand that is established at the end. The daily rate is achieved at the end of the flow process. This is compared with the scheduling and lead time techniques of traditional manufacturing. Product synchronization is a technique to show the relationship of the individual flow processes coming together to create the part or product. Thus, the flow process may resemble an inverse tree with individual processes, with assembly or machine cell branches feeding into the main flow at the points at which their components are needed.

Once the product synchronization is defined, each of the individual processes is broken into a TQC Sequence Of Events (SOE). Since the end of the process is given the highest priority for implementation, final assembly processes are targeted for starting points in defining the TQC sequence of events.

TQC Sequence of Events (SOE)

The TQC sequence of events is the first key element of a TQC flow process (reference Figure 3-2). It is the series of work content steps and quality criteria that need to be completed in order to manufacture the quality product. When doing a TQC sequence of events there is a natural tendency for traditional batch manufacturers to think in terms of batches, lumps or traditional subassemblies. This should be acknowledged and then avoided. Instead of thinking in terms of batches or subassemblies, the thought process should follow the natural flow of the product.

Categories of Work

The TQC sequence of events is a natural flow of the tasks required to create a product. The TQC sequence of events describes the sequential work and, most importantly, the quality criteria for each work step to manufacture the product. Each task in the sequence of events is classified in one of four categories of work. The four categories are:

1. Required labor work

2. Required machine work

3. Setup time

4. Move time

The quality requirements for each step are then identified. The primary objective—to produce the highest quality product, TQC— cannot be achieved until the manufacturer understands the specific work and the corresponding quality requirements essential to produce a product. Above all, the manufacturer must commit to taking quality to the people and machines that build the product. The path to total quality products is based upon the foundation of a total quality process.

In-Process Quality

W*orld-class* manufacturing is based upon a flow process in which the people and machines that build the product are given the involvement, responsibility, TQC tools, authority and methods to achieve their goal. Outdated and expensive external quality inspection techniques, although still practiced by many companies in the archaic defense industry as well as some other government-regulated industries, focus on external inspection tools and final product tests. Those antiquated practices ("We've always done it this way," or "We're unique") seem preferred over creating a TQC process that eliminates the initial opportunity to create a nonquality part or product. The responsibility of quality must start in design engineering and become a predominant focus at each step to build a product. Once the TQC sequence of events has been developed and the quality criteria defined, this flow of the product will then dictate the line layout. The associated work content time will also assist management in determining the number of machines and people required to produce the forecasted volumes of products.

Classification of Work

Every step to manufacture a product will be associated with one of the four categories of work. Work will be classified to ensure that the requirements to meet product specification are understood and met, and to prioritize improvement to the process. All steps to build a product will fall into one of those four categories of work. However, not all work will add value to the product or process, even though it must be completed in order for the customer's expectations and product specifications to be met.

Boost Value-Added Steps

Each step is also classified as a value- or nonvalue-added step. Value-added steps in the production process are those that increase the worth of a product or service to a customer or consumer. Value-added steps can only be determined by placing yourself in the "eyes" of your customer. It is essential to identify value-added steps as compared with steps that do not add value so that efforts can be made to increase the percentage of value-added steps and, wherever possible, to eliminate steps that do not add value. Sometimes that is not possible. As an example, in-process testing that is not required in your product specification is not value-added work, even though it is a good business decision to test—it is *preferable* because of process variables or material inconsistencies, but it is *not value-added*. The testing time work would fall under the setup time classification. Testing would be value-added if the customer required it to be part of your product's specification. The product needs to perform and provide dependable service to the customer, and testing is a way to prevent process and material defects from getting to the customer—but the testing itself does not add value.

Value-Added Limited to Required Labor/Machine Steps

Required labor time represents the required steps performed by people for the product to meet your advertised product specifications. While labor time is needed in order for the product to meet these specifications, not all labor time is value-added.

Required machine time also represents the essential steps performed by machines for the product to meet your specifications. Required machine time, like required labor time, may or may not add value to the product.

Move and Setup Add No Value

Move time is the time spent in moving products or materials through the process, from the point where they were produced or introduced to the point where they will be consumed. Move time may be either with labor or machine time. It is always nonvalue-added work. Appreciable move time is usually indicative of a poor line layout.

Setup time is work that is performed prior to required machine or labor time, and it, too, is always nonvalue-added. Setup time can range from changing a tool pack and making the necessary adjustments on a large machine to opening and removing a cable from a package. Once the nonvalue-added step is identified, modifications in packaging, line layout and

Product P/N ______ **DEMAND FLOW® TECHNOLOGY** Process I.D. ______

SEQ. #	TASK DESCRIPTION	V.A.	SET-UP		MACHINE	LABOR	MOVE		TQC INFORMATION
			M	L			M	L	

Figure 3-2 DFT/TQC Sequence of Events

machine setup procedures can often be made to reduce setup time.

Departure from Traditional Routing

The TQC sequence of events is quite different from a traditional product routing. The traditional product routing tends to be of a summary nature and typically includes operations for assembly, inspection, testing, setup time, move time and run time for both machine and labor. The traditional routing is useful in routing the product from work center to work center and in loading the planned hours in each traditional department or work center. The labor routing does not distinguish between a value- and nonvalue-added step. Thus, in conventional manufacturing there is no effective way to determine which steps should be targeted for elimination. The traditional router is used as a collection device to gather employee efficiency data or process performance data based upon the work order that has been scheduled. Most importantly, the traditional router does not contain the specific verification nor TQC criteria essential to a total quality process. Typically, a traditional router will direct the product or subassembly to go to inspection to be approved by an external inspector.

The TQC sequence of events in the flow process is a key element in the design of the fundamental flow process. It will be used as a basis to methodize the process; it will be used for total product cycle time calculation; and, it will point the way to process improvement via the identification of dangerous designed-for-defect steps and the elimination of nonvalue-added steps. Standard routings have little value in flow manufacturing and should not be used if a scheduling manufacturer is transitioning to *world-class* Demand Flow Technology. Compromises on establishing the quality flow process will affect the success of the overall project. Such compromise is often tied to a lack of understanding or commitment from the top management.

Total Time Calculations

Once the TQC sequence of events has been defined, the total time to build the product can be calculated. The sum of all machine, labor, setup and move sequences will be the total time to build the product. The total time to build the product is usually broken into total labor time and total machine time. This labor and machine time will be used to determine staffing and machine utilization in the manufacturing plant based on the daily rate to be achieved. All work content, value- and non-value-added, to build or machine a product added together will reveal the total labor and total machine time to create the product.

All of the value-added steps are required if the product is to meet the customer expectations and the manufacturer's specifications. It is natural to place all value-added steps in a cost category that charges them directly to product costs. The non-value-added steps are placed into a cost category regarding ineffective manufacturing costs. These ineffective product costs are not dictated by the customer requirements or product specification. These nonvalue-added steps contribute to higher product costs and lower profit margins. The relation of value-added time versus total time yields the following process efficiency formula:

$$Process\ Design\ Efficiency\ \% = \frac{VW}{TT}\ x\ 100$$

TT = Total Labor Time + Total Machine Time (VW + NV)

VW = Sum of the Value-Added Work Content (Machine and Labor) Time

NV = Sum of the Nonvalue-Added Work Content (Machine and Labor) Time

Management attention is focused on the elimination of nonvalue-added steps and the improvement of the process quality. As nonvalue-added steps are removed or reduced, the manufacturing process efficiency will increase.

Designing Work Content

Through the TQC sequence of events, we have identified the total work and total quality criteria to build a product. Once this is completed, the work content would ideally be grouped into equal pieces of work as we start designing a flow process. Under ideal conditions, each piece would require exactly the same length of work content time. An ideal layout of the entire production process, including the line, feeders and machine cells, would hopefully show each process cut into equal pieces of work content time. If it took a total of 16 hours to create a product and such production was achieved by 32 increments of 30 minutes each, the pull process of flow manufacturing would function smoothly, perhaps perfectly, completing a product every 30 minutes.

However, since most processes are dominated by non-perfect people and dissimilar machines, an absolute synchronization *cannot* be achieved. Therefore, a series of balancing techniques has been developed for flow manufacturing. These techniques have the effect of "equalizing" the pieces of work. They enable shaping the relationship of processes and coordinating the elements of work content. Operational cycle time, the Takt of the process, and flow balancing techniques, which drive the design of the entire process, are two of those techniques.

Line Design for Flow Manufacturing

Designed daily rate (capacity) and the corresponding flow targets must be established for each product to be manufactured. This targeted rate (capacity) is based upon a marketing and top-management agreement. Normally, flow lines are designed, one time, at the highest required rate (capacity). Usually, that is a volume that cannot be surpassed unless a second or third shift is utilized or unless the work week is stretched from five to six or seven days. Although they are designed at one volume, which is capacity, flow manufacturing lines are flexible and can easily run well below that volume. Based upon actual demand and without redesigning the line or changing a single production method sheet, the range of volumes produced will be between the designed maximum volume and 50 percent of that volume. To calculate the designed daily rate, divide the targeted monthly volume by the number of work days in the month:

$$Dcp = \frac{Pv}{Wd}$$

Dcp = Designed Daily Rate (Capacity)

Pv = Targeted Monthly Volume

Wd = Work Days Per Month

This will provide the targeted number of units to be produced per day as the designed daily rate. As an example, if the designed monthly plan is based upon 500 units and the total number of work days per month is 20, the designed daily rate would be 25 units per day. Although the daily rate can and will be adjusted a little every day, flow lines are designed one time at the capacity volume.

Flow rates are tools used in the design as well as the daily management of a flow process. They are based on actual daily units completed at the back of the flow process. In the flow rate calculation, the use of effective work hours, or the amount of time that can be anticipated as actual work time, is required. As a typical example, production employees work a standard 8 1/2-hour day with allowances for a 30-minute lunch, and two 15-minute breaks. The remaining work time is then factored down between 12 and 18 minutes a day to allow for quality discussions and personal time. Based upon this example, the effective work hours would be 7.3. The flow line flow rate is equal to the specific daily rate divided by the effective work hours times the number of shifts per day:

$$Fr = \frac{Dr}{H(S)}$$

Fr   =   Daily Flow Rate

Dr   =   Daily Rate

H   =   Effective Work Hours

S   =   Work Shifts Per Day

Thus, a daily rate of 50 units divided by 7.3 hours in a one-shift operation would yield a flow rate of 6.8 units per hour. If all other things were equal and the daily rate of 50 units was achieved from a plant operating with two shifts, the flow rate would be half that, or approximately 3.4 units per hour. The calculation would be 50 divided by 7.3 times 2, or 50 divided by 14.6. Flow rates are important in managing the progress throughout the day, particularly in the high-volume manufacturing processes. They are always monitored at the end of a product line.

Operational Cycle Time

Operational cycle time is based upon the designed daily rate or capacity. It is the targeted work-content time required for a single person or machine to produce a single part or product within the flow process. The Operational Cycle time calculation establishes the "Takt" (rhythm or beat) of the process. It is a calculated, numeric time value and it is based on the *targeted* work content. Operational cycle time is the reciprocal relationship of the flow rate. It is shown as:

$$OP \; c/t = \frac{H(S)}{Dcp}$$

H   =   Effective Work Hours

S   =   Work Shifts Per Day

Dcp =   Designed Daily Rate (Capacity)

Thus, simply stated, the operational cycle time equals the effective work hours in a shift multiplied by the number of shifts per day and divided by the designed daily rate capacity. With the daily rate of 5 and 7.3 effective work hours per shift, the one-shift operation would have an operational cycle time or Takt of 1.46 hours per unit or, as preferably stated in minutes, 87.6 minutes per unit.

The operational cycle time formulas or calculations would be used for all flow manufacturing lines, regardless of the product or volume. The targeted work content is identified based upon the operational cycle time calculation. The TQC sequence of events is then grouped into pieces of work equal to this targeted work content. These ideally equal, grouped pieces of work are defined as a flow operation.

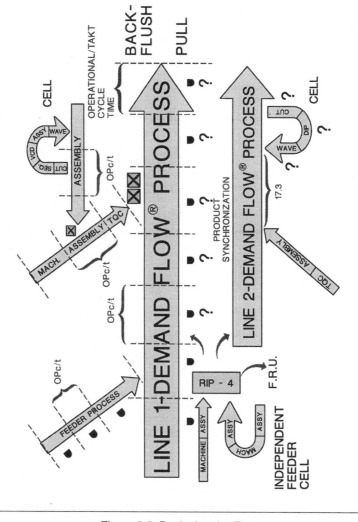

Figure 3-3 Designing the Flow

Targeted Rate, C/T Relationships

In conclusion—the higher the designed daily rate or the higher the volume required, the shorter the designed operational cycle time, the faster the Takt; the lower the designed daily rate or volume required, the longer the designed operational cycle time, the slower the Takt. These designed daily rates of products to be produced will determine the corresponding work content required to achieve this targeted rate or volume. Once the targeted work is defined, the TQC sequence of events will be independently grouped into machine and labor operations. Each operation would ideally have actual work content equal to the targeted cycle time of the production line or cell.

Volume Adjustments: People

This designed operational work content and corresponding TQC quality criteria is now defined and basically fixed. To adjust the volume of products required to meet specific rates, either people will be removed from the operations and machines turned off or fewer hours will be worked per day, but the operational work content and corresponding quality criteria is not changed. As an example, the actual volume of products produced may simply be reduced by 50 percent from the designed daily rate (capacity) by removing every other person and turning off the appropriate machines. The flexible production employees simply move from operation to operation, but the work content and the quality criteria at each operation is *not* changed. The flexible production employees are invaluable elements in the flow manufacturing processes, and their certification, reward and compensation should reflect their new responsibilities and contributions.

Line Design

In flow manufacturing, production lines or cells are always designed at the highest required rate and the corresponding shortest required cycle time. When designing a flow line or cell, the manufacturer should seek the anticipated capacity volumes for each particular product from top management and marketing. This required volume must look forward at least a year into the foreseeable future. The flow manufacturer will then calculate the targeted operational cycle time based upon this anticipated highest rate to establish the Takt of the line. The manufacturer will then design a line with operational work and quality criteria equal to the corresponding Takt time.

Rate Changes, Line Does Not

As discussed earlier, it is not necessary to change a line layout every time a required rate is changed. The flexible employee in the flow process will enable lines to run at lower rates by removing employees from required operations. A line or cell with fewer production employees than the total number of operations is known as a "line with a 'hole' in it." Production employees will move from operation to operation to maintain the pull process. Employees removed from the line will work on employee involvement tasks, cross-training and quality improvement programs until the higher volume of products is again required. The "holes" in the flow line will move up and down the line as production employees move to pull work to each operation.

Imbalances Possible

Once the targeted rates and corresponding Takt times have been defined and the actual operational work content is established, there may be an imbalance between the target operational cycle time and the actual observed operational cycle time. Operations that are labor intensive can be adjusted by relocating material or work content between operations to give people more or less work. However, operations involving machines that effectively run at one speed require different techniques to adjust for the imbalance.

Adjusting for Line Imbalances

The objective is to have the actual work content equal to the targeted operational cycle time. Refer to Figure 3-4 and consider a flow line where five successive operations have an actual work content as follows:

Operation 30, 21.5 Minutes

Operation 40, 20.0 Minutes

Operation 50, 20.0 Minutes

Operation 60, 25.0 Minutes

Operation 70, 20.0 Minutes

These operations are part of a flow line that is designed to produce 22 units per day. However, Operation 60 is a machine operation that produces a unit every 25 minutes—no more, no less. The calculation of targeted operational cycle time:

$$OP \ c/t = \frac{H(S)}{Dcp} \ \frac{7.3(1)}{22} = .33 \ Hour = 20 \ Minutes$$

OP c/t	=	Targeted Operational Cycle Time
H	=	Effective Work Hours
S	=	Shifts Per Day
Dcp	=	Designed Daily Rate (Capacity)

The targeted cycle time of this line is 20 minutes, but the actual time to produce a part at Operation 60 is 25 minutes. During the 7.3-hour day, the 20-minute operations would produce 22 parts, while the 25-minute operations would produce only about 17 units. Since the line is targeting a rate of 22 units per day and the machine at Operation 60 is only capable of producing 17 units per shift, the manufacturer would basically have three alternatives to solve this imbalance problem:

1. Reduce the cycle time of the machine at Operation 60 to 20 minutes by eliminating any nonvalue-added time, such as setup or move time;

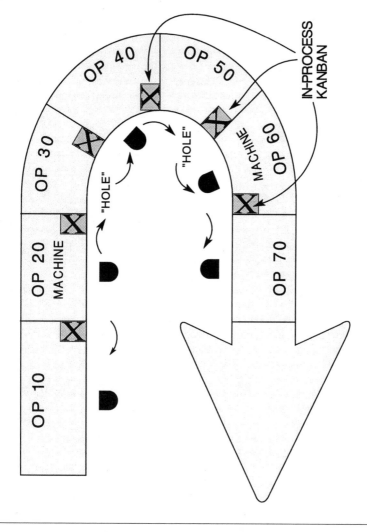

Figure 3-4 Flow Line with "Hole"

2. Obtain an additional machine capable of producing at least five units per shift;

3. Create an inventory of units around the machine that would allow the machine to run longer hours than the remainder of the line.

Although the first alternative is always preferred, and the second alternative is usually the most expensive, the third alternative becomes the most common choice. The number of units—inventory—required to allow the machine to work additional hours is computed based upon the imbalance between the actual time to produce a part and the targeted cycle time of the process.

$$\frac{In\text{--}process\ Kanban}{(Inventory)} = \frac{Imbalance\ x\ Cycles\ of\ Imbalance}{Operational\ Cycle\ Time}$$

During the 7.3-hour first shift, there would be a buildup of five units between Operation 50 and Operation 60. The machine could work additional time on a second shift processing the buildup of five parts to Operation 70 for the start of the next day. At the start of the next day, the inventory in the front of Operation 60 would be zero and in front of Operation 70 would be five units. This inventory, required to support the imbalance, is referred to as an in-process Kanban (reference Figure 3-4). Cost of another machine notwithstanding, the imbalance does not appear sufficient to warrant one.

Overtime or Additional Shifts as Tools

Based upon the imbalance of units, additional hours of production are needed. They could be provided through a second shift or by alternating operators and keeping the machine running through lunch and breaks. An in-process Kanban containing several units would exist before the machine and before Operation 70. This in-process Kanban would contain the units produced in overtime or on the second shift, and it would keep the line flowing and achieve the targeted daily rate. If the imbalance was caused by a setup or nonvalue-added work, that problem could be attacked vigorously. If the work content cannot be balanced, then this imbalance between two operations is handled with an in-process Kanban, a point of supply between the two, sized to equalize the imbalance.

Equalizing the Process

The objective in flow line design is for work content to be equal to the targeted operational cycle time. Once this is understood, it is quite possible, as an example, for an automobile manufacturer and an ordinary pencil manufacturer to have the same targeted operational cycle time. If eight automobiles were to be produced in an eight-hour day and eight pencils were to be produced in an eight-hour day, both would have the same operational cycle time—one hour. However, there would probably be many more people working on the automobiles than on the pencils. The targeted operational cycle time would be the same, but the number of people and machines would differ.

People in the Process

The operational cycle time defines the targeted work content for each operation. This calculation establishes the Takt for each process. Barring a change or improvement to the process and after the line is designed, the operational work content is fixed, and it is no longer rate sensitive. The number of people required to support a process is based upon the labor time per unit—it is very rate sensitive. Consider a process that has a daily rate of 25 units per shift, total labor hours from the TQC sequence of events of 36.0 hours per unit, and effective work hours in a shift of 7.3.

People needed to support the process is derived by multiplying the specific product daily rate by its total labor hours per unit and then dividing by the effective work hours in a shift which is multiplied by the number of shifts:

$$People\ In\text{-}process\ =\ \frac{DxL}{H(S)}\quad \frac{25\ x\ 36.0}{7.3(1)}\ =\ 124\ People$$

D   =   Specific Daily Rate Quantity

L   =   Labor Time from the TQC Sequence of Events

H   =   Effective Work Hours

S   =   Number of Shifts Per Day

The process requires 124 people. If the line is not running at its designed capacity, there will be "holes" in the line. The

people simply move from operation to operation upon completion of the work content at their primary operation.

These are techniques that would be used to design and
balance a flow line. And, once the rate and cycle time techniques
have been mastered, along with an understanding of the pull
techniques, the particular product or related technology used to
produce it are irrelevant.

Total Product Cycle Time

Total product cycle time (TP c/t) is the next key element
of the production flow process that will be calculated. TP c/t is
the calculated longest path of a flow process as measured from
the completion of the product. This is a key value that will be
the basis for the inventory investment dictated by the process.
It will also be the basis for absorption of overhead in the flow
manufacturing financial system. Improvements in the process
will be listed in priority along this path with the intent of
eliminating nonvalue-added steps. Total product cycle time is
basically a fixed number that is not rate sensitive and will not
change as long as the process is stable. Elimination of nonvalue-added steps along the TP c/t path will cause the path to
move around and change the focus for process improvement
activities. Total product cycle time is calculated as the work
content through the longest path of the process to build the
product.

Starting from the End

In the flow manufacturing pull process, the daily rate is achieved at the completion, or end, of the flow process. The last operation pulls from the previous operation and all the way through to the calculated origin of the product. In the calculation of TP c/t, the end of the line is always the starting point of the measurement (reference Figure 3-5). Starting from the end working up the flow line to the calculated beginning, the TP c/t path can be determined by taking the longest step at each of the many decision points in the process. Each of those steps represents a discussion or analysis on which path with respective offshoots is the longest. By beginning at shipping, going back through the production process and moving off to feeder and other side or main processes, the longest path can be determined. It is the longest, cumulative, single path back through the process, regardless of whether it follows the main line or trails off to a feeder process.

Once the total product cycle time has been determined, steps can be taken to shorten it. Based upon an improvement to the steps in the process, this path can and will move. Focus must be maintained on total product cycle time. And, nonvalue-added steps, such as setups and move time, can be analyzed for reduction. Total product cycle time is not rate sensitive, and it does not change unless there are improvements to the production flow process.

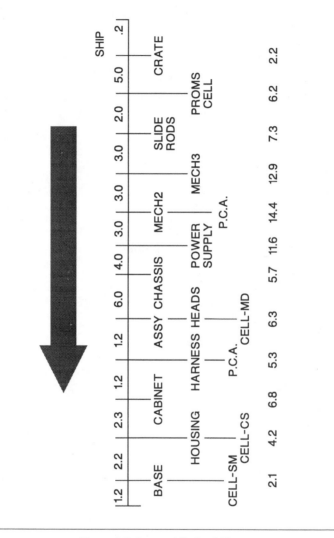

Figure 3-5 Longest Path of Flow

Analysis of Flow Path

Analysis of the flow path (total product cycle time) always begins at the completion, or end, of the process. The analysis involves taking the work content, adding back to front at the point in the process where the first feeder is consumed or required for final assembly. Adding the work content time from the back of the process to the point where the feeder is consumed plus the work content time of the feeder process will yield the time through the first feeder. The analysis continues from the back to the next point where a second feeder process is consumed. Work content time from the back of the process to the point where this feeder is consumed, plus the work content time of this feeder process is added and compared to the work content time calculated for the previous feeder. The feeder process associated with the lowest number is eliminated as the analysis continues to each point where a feeder process is consumed. The search is for the longest path as measured in time. This will be the total product cycle time required by the flow of the process.

Backtracking

As an example, consider a process that has three feeders with total time of each feeder being: (#1) 12 minutes, (#2) 20 minutes, and (#3) 32 minutes, respectively (reference Figure 3-6).

Feeder process #3 is consumed last in the sequence of events. It is consumed, and after that, 12 minutes of additional work content is done up to the point of shipping. Therefore, the path through this feeder is 32 minutes plus 12 minutes, or 44 minutes. Feeder #2 is needed next, and 30 minutes of work is done after it is consumed. Therefore, the path through feeder process #2 is 30 minutes plus 20 minutes, or 50 minutes. Since this value is greater than the 44 minutes calculated for feeder process #3, feeder process #3 is eliminated from further consideration. Feeder process #1 is consumed first with 35 minutes work being done after it is consumed. Therefore, the path through feeder #1 is 35 minutes plus 12, or 47 minutes. This also is shorter than the 50 minutes for feeder process #2, so it, too, is eliminated. Thus, for this process, the total product cycle time through the longest path is 50 minutes, and it would be through feeder process #2.

Dictates Inventory Investment

Total product cycle time is of crucial importance in the Demand Flow process for three primary reasons. First, it dictates the minimal inventory investment required to support the process. The shorter the total product cycle time, the shorter the amount of time that inventory must be on hand in the production process. In traditional subassembly manufacturing (MRP II), in-process inventory is maintained for the lead time days, weeks or months that it takes to schedule, queue, kit and build each level of the multilevel product. In Demand Flow manufacturing, the product can progress through the flow process in less than the total work content hours to build the product. Also, as the total product cycle time is reduced, so too is the corresponding in-process inventory investment.

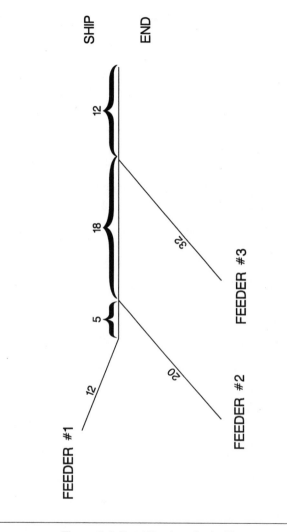

Figure 3-6 Total Product Cycle Time

Basis for Overhead Absorption

Secondly, total product cycle time is crucial because it is the basis for the application of overhead. The efficient Demand Flow manufacturer will not apply overhead based upon labor since it is not a primary point of focus and since it is the smallest and a shrinking portion of product cost. Total product cycle time is a consistent and fixed basis for the application of overhead. As total product cycle time is reduced, overhead is not fully absorbed. Pressure is applied to management and marketing to focus on additional products or to enable additional volume to be supported in the process with the same overhead. Traditionally, underabsorption of overhead is a negative feature. It can mean that an insufficient number of labor hours (inventory) have been produced to meet the budget. This can cause the inventory to be built up to absorb the overhead. In Demand Flow manufacturing, the underabsorption of overhead, because of the reduction of the total product cycle time, can be a powerful management tool to force process improvements.

Guide for Improvement

The third primary purpose of total product cycle time is that it serves as a guide for the process improvement program. The priority of the process improvement/employee involvement program should be emphasized along the TP c/t path of the process. The *world-class* Demand Flow manufacturer must strive to reduce nonvalue-added steps in order to reduce the inventory investment time and reduce total product cycle time along with the corresponding absorption of overhead.

Increasing Inventory Turns

The in-process inventory investment in Demand Flow manufacturing is dictated by the total product cycle time. Reducing total product cycle time is a primary objective. Total product cycle time is determined by the work content along the longest path of the process, which is usually a shorter period of time than the total work content, or the total amount of time it takes to build a product. As an example and using an oversimplified line layout, the total time it takes to build a product may be 20 hours. That may include an 8-hour feeder process that is consumed towards the end of the line. If the consuming line is a totally sequential process of one step after another for 12 hours, the longest path could be 12 hours if the 8-hour feeder process occurred simultaneously. Even though it takes 20 total hours to build the product, parts and raw materials—all inventory—need only be in the process for 12 work hours. Shortening the total product cycle time to reduce the time inventory must be present, and increasing the material turnover is a primary objective and goal from a financial standpoint.

Single-digit inventory turns are no longer acceptable, and they can cripple a corporation's competitive power. Traditional techniques, methods utilizing the schedule-based formal systems (MRP II), will produce traditional results. Achieving competitive goals of 24 to 26 inventory turns annually as a minimum will require nontraditional techniques and systems.

Developing the Competitive Edge

Demand Flow Technology becomes the foundation for the *world-class* corporation. Business strategies take advantage of the quality and customer-responsive benefits to dominate markets and industries. TQC sequence of events, total product cycle time, operational cycle time, and method sheets are tools and techniques necessary for developing the basis for a flow production process—Demand Flow Technology. These techniques and formulas will become the basis for a Demand Flow production process. The process should begin with identifying the natural product flow, work content, corresponding quality criteria, and nonvalue-added steps through the sequence of events process. Then, the operational cycle time will be calculated based upon the highest required rate. Operational method sheets will be created to identify work content and quality criteria graphically at an operation based upon the targeted operational cycle time. Total product cycle time will then be calculated as a guide to inventory investment, overhead absorption and process improvement. By identifying these essential building blocks of a Demand Flow process, the *world-class* manufacturer has the framework for a powerful, competitive tool. With the additional market pressure from powerful new competitors, in addition to the shortened product life cycles, these techniques will become essential to industry leaders of the 1990s where *speed-to-market will dictate profit and market share.*

Chapter Four

Customer Responsiveness and Linear Planning

S urvival and eventual success is based upon product acceptance and customer sales. Without the customer sales, the
product and corporation goals become a mere dream. Competitive markets will require successful corporations to become
increasingly responsive to changes in customer demand. Immediate response to fluctuations in product volumes and model
mixes are key elements of a Demand Flow process.

Linear planning and material forecasting are the techniques
that will determine the production volumes required to satisfy
the anticipated demand of products a customer will buy and
when those products will be bought. They also enable the
transition from lumpy, infrequent and inaccurate forecasts to a
linear, daily production plan. The primary tools are Market

Flexibility, Total Product Cycle Time, Forecast Consumption Techniques, Demand Time Fences, and Planning Flexibility Fences. These tools also draw together historic antagonists in manufacturing. Sales, marketing, materials, production, and product planning will work on a much more cooperative basis in Demand Flow manufacturing and come up with better forecasts and plans in a more manageable system.

Traditionally Long Lead Times

The goal of the *world-class* manufacturer is to deliver high-quality products to the customer on a timely basis while minimizing the inventory investment and keeping the production process as linear and as flexible as possible. In traditional scheduled manufacturing there typically is a fixed, long lead time for purchased material. Once traditional manufacturers place orders with suppliers, traditional suppliers must then procure adequate material and produce their products to meet consuming manufacturers' demand. Thus, the supplier's lead time, which includes its scheduling, queue and production time, must be added to the consuming manufacturer's lead time, which also includes its scheduling, queue and production time before the ultimate customer can be served (reference Figure 4-1).

Targeting Customer Responsiveness

In linear Demand Flow manufacturing, a long-term purchasing/planning forecast is shared with the suppliers. This forecast allows the supplier to plan material and production processes. In exchange for this longer-term forecast, the supplier reduces fixed lead times to the consuming Demand Flow manufacturer. Thus, the supplier's lead time is reduced to the very short production time needed to make the supplied part. The supplier's short production time, plus the Demand Flow manufacturer's total product cycle time, becomes the manufacturing lead time. With the very long lead time associated with traditional scheduled manufacturing, the customer must either wait a long time to receive product, or the manufacturer will buffer its forecasting errors with inventory. The inventory will be in the form of either finished goods, purchased parts or work-in-process. As the total product cycle times and flexibility lead times with the suppliers are reduced, a departure is made from the typical finished goods business to the made-to-order business. The inventory investment is reduced—customer responsiveness and service will be increased.

In scheduled manufacturing, traditionally and frequently what happens is that the product demand will spike. Production will be asked to go from its current production volumes to a much higher volume in a short period of time. Traditional schedules are increased to reflect the higher quantities. Demand Flow manufacturing practitioners also strive to meet the revenue plan both in forecast and in dollars and with the associated option mix—but in a non-spiked, controlled fashion. Daily rates are continuously being increased or decreased gradually to follow the customer demand and to meet the revenue and forecast plan. The objective is to achieve the targeted revenue

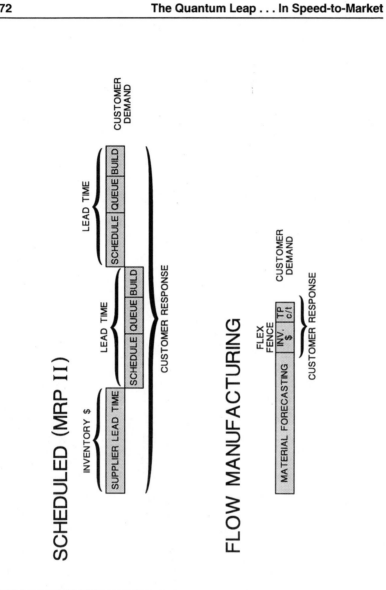

Figure 4-1 Customer Responsiveness

and forecast plan in a customer-responsive and controlled fashion.

Small Changes Allowed

In a Demand Flow manufacturing environment, marketing is able to make many small changes in a short period of time. The goal for all organizations in the company—marketing, materials, production planning, production—is to meet the market-driven demands while minimizing inventory investment and keeping the production process as linear as possible. The result of the blend of these different factors in a consistent fashion is a very powerful manufacturing process facilitated by the flexible Demand-Based production plan. Elements of the master plan include forecast consumption techniques, demand time fences, planning flex fences, actual orders, production capacity, finished goods management, the product option mix, and the products available to promise to the customer.

Demand Flow Is Market-Driven

Many people, particularly in manufacturing, have joked for many years about the accuracy or inaccuracy of the marketing forecast; the term "accurate forecast" has been labelled as an oxymoron. The two types of marketing forecasts have been called "lucky" and "lousy" or "bad" and "worse." Forecasts that do not turn into actual customer orders become burdensome inventory, either as components or as finished goods. Understated forecasts eventually turn into shortages, if not for a particular order pulled up, then for orders to be pulled in the future. The typical relationship of the number of orders shipped early due to a pull-up, and the number of orders shipped late due to a pull-up is (L = orders shipped late; P = orders pulled up):

$$L = P^2$$

In defense of marketing, it is a department burdened by customers who sometimes do not know how much of what they will be needing. When they do know, they sometimes keep that information from the marketing organization. Additionally, marketing can be hamstrung by a manufacturing organization and production process that can be unresponsive, attributing to poor customer satisfaction levels. The key in Demand Flow manufacturing is to get the manufacturing and marketing organizations together to negotiate a requirements plan for a product that can be achieved in a linear fashion by manufacturing. This plan must also meet the marketing needs as determined by the customers. This is accomplished through the Demand-Based production planning process.

The production process was designed at a capacity volume which corresponds to the lowest required operational cycle time. Typically, it is not necessary to change line layout or production processes to make the many small changes necessary to respond to the fluctuating marketing plan. If the changes become larger than the production process can support (more than 30 percent above planned capacity or less than 50 percent of the designed volume), then, through the planning process, it can be determined how to make the changes in the flow line. Otherwise you must return to marketing for further negotiations.

Marketing/Manufacturing Alliance

Customer and supplier involvements are paramount in developing a flexible manufacturing plan for a company using Demand Flow Technology. The forecasts of marketing, heavily punctuated by change and more change, become a flexible Demand-Based plan. On the one hand, the flow manufacturing process is market driven. On the other hand, the flow manufacturing process must maintain a rein on the flexibility associated with the marketing forecasts. Marketing is asked to take responsibility for finished goods inventory—not physically, but in terms of inventory management and accountability. That is because under Demand Flow Technology and its Demand-Based planning process, any finished goods inventory most likely comes about as a result of an order from marketing which was not supported by a corresponding customer order. Marketing must figure out what the customer is going to want and assist manufacturing in what they should do to satisfy that demand. Manufacturing will press for forecast accuracy within certain parameters, but, more significantly, it must provide assistance in the effort.

Demand Flow Technology Preferred by Marketing

Top management and marketing personnel tend to prefer Demand Flow Technology for three reasons:

- First, the product goes through the production process in a much shorter period of time.

- Second, in Demand Flow manufacturing the production process is very flexible which allows many small changes to the production plan to be accommodated in a very short period of time. These are not major changes, but many small adjustments. No manufacturing process, including Demand Flow manufacturing, can go up or down as fast as marketing might like, but the greater flexibility of Demand Flow manufacturing can represent a significant marketing tool. In traditional manufacturing there is a tendency to freeze the production plan for a month, a quarter, and, in some cases, even longer. This ties the hands of marketing in terms of making more sales to customers or manipulating finished goods in a desired or advantageous fashion.

- Third, under Demand Flow manufacturing, high-quality products come out of the Demand Flow process in the manner and time intended. In traditional manufacturing, there is a tendency to make the majority of the monthly or quarterly goal at the end of the production month or quarter. Therefore, customers who requested product at the initial and middle stages of the month have little chance of obtaining their requested product delivery.

Total Customer Satisfaction

Customer service measures are traditionally monitored on a monthly basis. Thus, if a product is shipped on the 31st of a month when it was due on the 15th, it is considered an on-time delivery by the manufacturer, even though it is two weeks late in the eyes of the customer. In Demand Flow manufacturing, linear manufacturing and making the daily rate in a linear fashion will aid in getting products to customers when and as promised. It is a very predictable process which means that instead of selling quality problems or shipping delays to the customer, marketing can concentrate on new or expanded business. Marketing not only has the ability to make small changes in a short period of time to meet customer demand, but also is selling products that are made at a higher level of quality due to the quality being built into the TQC production process. Marketing also gets the powerful tool of faster and more timely delivery. From a manufacturing standpoint, extreme peaks and valleys in demand are removed. Manufacturing cannot and should not be requested to go from two units one day to ten units the next day. But it can go from two units to three units and from three units per day to four units, until reaching the desired volume over a controlled period of time.

Quicker Response

Traditional scheduled manufacturing may take 24 to 36 weeks in accumulated lead time to deliver a product that can be delivered with Demand Flow manufacturing techniques in a matter of days. The major difference is the elimination of lead time and other such traditional creatures as scheduling, planning and queuing at every operation. Demand Flow manufacturing does not recognize traditional manufacturing lead time techniques. In Demand Flow manufacturing, suppliers are given a long-term planning forecast to assist in their planning visibility. The supplier is given the long-term planning forecast which is long before the time a purchase order would have been released under conventional manufacturing. This gives the supplier a far greater "jump" on meeting the Demand Flow manufacturer's requirements without the need for long lead times or causing delays in meeting the targeted production date.

In a Demand-Based planning process, marketing and manufacturing will negotiate a Demand-Based production rate for each product. The corresponding output of the production process will then be calculated for the product or group of products. A range of flexible volumes will be negotiated with suppliers for the delivery of supporting material. Only then can the synchronization of the marketing-negotiated volume, the daily production volume, and the flexibility with the suppliers be managed in a consistent manner. Within a very short period of time, no less than the manufacturing total product cycle time, no changes will be made to this production plan. Outside this short fixed interval (TP c/t), planning flexibility will be negotiated with production, marketing and eventually the suppliers.

Three Masters

Business discussions related to pricing, market share, costs and product volume should be developed around a consistent strategy. This strategy is based upon the synchronization between the three masters of production: marketing, suppliers and the manufacturing process itself. Marketing must not promise what suppliers and their production process cannot deliver or to a delivery time that cannot be met. There is no need for the process to deliver goods that marketing cannot sell. There is no need to get materials from the supplier too soon or too late to serve marketing. Coordination and synchronization of the three masters occur through the art of negotiation. Demand Flow Technology links the three masters inseparably together in a methodology referred to as Demand-Based Management.

Initial Determinations for Plan

Some information must be developed and preliminary decisions made prior to beginning Demand-Based planning. One such piece of information is the manufacturing calendar: what days are to be worked, the number of shifts, the effective work hours, and the annual holidays. The nature of the product must also be analyzed with an eye toward delivery policy considerations in the Demand-Based production plan. Is this a product that the market will wait for, such as a custom automobile or other major products often built to customer order with a wide assortment of options? If the market will wait, how long will it wait? If it is a product that the market will not wait for—a product, such as a toaster or telephone—the products must be readily available, or the customer will immediately turn to a competitor. If finished goods are dictated, building-to-stock and monitoring finished goods inventory for quantity and option mix must be considered. With build-to-stock products, finished goods replenishment orders are the same to the manufacturing process as a customer order. However, the final determination of whether units should be shipped to finished goods or to a customer, or whether to shut down the production line, is largely a function of top management and marketing. As the Demand Flow manufacturing total product cycle time continues to come down, a transition toward a made-to-order manufacturing environment occurs. Finished goods inventory can then be reduced or eliminated.

Undercapacity Planning

In a Demand-Based planning environment, there are several advantages to planning at a level under manufacturing capacity:

- It is difficult to emphasize quality in a process that is running at full capacity. In the TQC process, employees utilize total quality control techniques to perform quality verification steps in addition to the typical production work. Quality is the number one objective, and it is never compromised in a TQC process. Verification and TQC steps are performed as top priority along with the work itself.

- It also enables the accomplishment of a major objective of Demand Flow manufacturing: that the production process becomes linear and that the daily rate be achieved every day—no more, no less.

- Running at undercapacity allows for training and employee involvement. This enables the employees to learn additional operations and encourages them to train for even more flexibility.

Other advantages include time for machine and equipment maintenance, process improvements, cleanup of the plant, and conducting meetings on employee involvement and quality.

If the daily rate is made approximately 7.0 or 7.5 hours for an 8-hour shift, the balance of the shift should be used for the purposes outlined above. If the daily rate is met in substantially less time than that, 6.0 or 6.5 hours into the shift, as an example, there may be too many people in the process or the calculation of requirement or of the actual capacity may be misstated. In either case, a review should be made; adjustments may be necessary. Of course, if necessary, the Demand Flow process can run at full, 100 percent capacity for short periods, but that should be discouraged for lengthy periods.

Demand-Based Planning

While traditional manufacturing usually schedules for the month, Demand Flow manufacturing executes a Demand-Based plan for each day. The Demand Flow manufacturing

Demand-Based plan is a specific, calculable number, and it is output as three elements:

1. The required daily rate

2. The targeted flow rate

3. The number of people or hours of machine time in each process

If any two elements are known, the other can be calculated. The information can be used to determine the corresponding flow rate of a process, the number of people needed to support a specific daily rate, or the maximum daily rate that a process can support. If one of the elements becomes variable, the impact on the other two variables can be analyzed. For example, if the required rate goes up, the additional people needed in the process to support the higher rate can be calculated as well as the lower observed flow rate needed to reach the higher rate. In the Demand Flow manufacturing process, the observed flow rate of units coming out of the back of the process is managed and charted.

Tracking Shorter Periods

The Demand Flow process will reach a point where a unit can be expected to be completed out of the process at the targeted flow rate. Management reporting evolves, as an example, from tracking 420 units per month down to the level of expecting one completed TQC unit every 21.9 minutes. The inability to achieve the daily rate points to a problem in the design or balance of a process.

Forecast Control Chart

The Demand-Based planning process begins with sessions between production and marketing aimed at negotiating a production volume for each product in the process. This negotiated volume can and will change over time, but initially it becomes the base level, a critical number for the application of demand and planning flex fences. Some companies build products totally to order. They do not have to worry about a forecast from marketing because it is a totally made-to-order environment. However, this is rare. Other make-to-stock companies don't use actual orders from marketing—they build strictly to a forecast. They are not concerned with actual orders coming from the customer. Most companies do require a forecast, at least for the material planning aspects of the process. Most manufacturers have to blend the forecast and the actual orders in their process—primarily manufacturing to customer orders but buying material to a forecast.

Marketing's Call

The term "forecast consumption" refers to the blending of the forecast and actual orders in a manner acceptable to both manufacturing and marketing. The premise behind forecast consumption is that marketing has a specific period of time to book or commit a customer order into the manufacturing process. If they pass that time, which is referred to as the demand time fence, then they will lose any forecasted quantities for that product that are greater than the actual customer orders at that particular point. If marketing still believes that a customer order will come in at the last minute, after the date it goes inside the demand time fence, then marketing will be allowed to place a finished goods replenishment order. These products associated with the finished goods replenishment order will go into a finished goods area and become "the property" of marketing. If the customer order does come in, then the product can be shipped on time. If not, marketing becomes "owner" of the inventory until it can be sold. It becomes marketing's call at that point—just outside the demand time fence—whether that inventory risk is appropriate and/or whether or not the customer commitment will come in for that order. The length of the demand time fence is typically between the total product cycle time and the quoted lead time of a product to a customer. The duration of the demand time fence may also include administrative response time and paperwork processing time.

Forecast/Orders to Actual Orders

If, as an example, a commitment is made to the customer that from the time the order is placed to the time of shipment is three weeks, then the demand time fence must appear at three weeks or less. Marketing then has until the third week to consume or book orders against the forecast. Once inside that fence, manufacturing is building strictly to orders that have already been received from the customer or for finished goods replenishment orders based upon marketing's high degree of confidence in their projection to turn the forecast into actual customer orders. The formal planning system should automatically cut back to actual orders inside the demand time fence. But if the order has not been received at that point, it is assumed that the order will not be received.

Thus, by definition of the demand time fence, only actual customer and finished goods replenishment orders are considered for the calculation of total demand. Outside the demand time fence, the greater of the forecast or actual orders is considered to be total demand. In most cases, that will be the forecast. If the actual orders outside the demand time fence are greater than the forecasted quantity, then the order quantity will be used for total demand with recognition that marketing has over booked the forecast for that particular period and an adjustment to forecast will be necessary.

Total Demand

The definition of total demand inside the demand time fence is the sum of actual customer and finished goods replenishment orders. Total demand outside the demand time fence is the greater of the forecast and actual customer orders. Therefore, the first step in the calculation of developing the production plan is to determine the total demand based upon the forecast consumption technique. The forecast consumption technique is applied against the forecast and actual orders to determine total demand. For example, if there is a 100-units-per-week forecast in the fifth week and actual orders of 105 units per week in the fifth week, the total demand would not pick up the forecast of the 100 but would pick up the actual customer orders of 105, thereby calculating a total demand of 105 units (reference Figure 4-2). In the first week, which is inside the demand time fence of one week, there may be actual customer orders of 100, but a forecast of 120 units. The total demand in the first week would be for 100 units unless marketing decides to give production a finished goods sales order for up to 20 units for the balance of the forecasted units.

Fence Governs

Unless marketing decides to buy the unsold units into finished goods, the 120-unit forecast would be overridden, since it is inside the demand time fence, and only the 100 units actually booked as customer orders would be acknowledged. In the third week, which is now outside the demand time fence, a forecast of 120 units with customer orders of 100 units would be treated differently: the 120 forecasted units would be taken as total demand since it was outside the demand time fence and it is the greater of the forecast versus actual orders. The total demand calculation is the basis of demand and planning time fences.

In developing the master production plan, a blend of forecasts and orders is used initially on a total demand control chart that is fixed only for a short time. Then, the limits of the chart reflect the flexibility parameters of material and capacity. A

	WEEK 1	WEEK 2	WEEK 3	WEEK 4	WEEK 5	WEEK 6
FORECAST :	120	105	120	135	100	120
ACTUAL ORDERS :	100	100	100	115	105	75
TOTAL DEMAND :	100	105	120	135	105	120

TP c/t

Figure 4-2 Calculating Total Demand

demand time fence, planning flex fences, linearity and mixed-model sequencing considerations are crucial to master plan development. It is also of critical importance that quantities which the process and suppliers can support be negotiated with marketing. Giving 20 percent flexibility to marketing while getting only 10 percent flexibility from suppliers is a shortcut to disaster. Nor can 20 units be promised to marketing when only five are in-process for the same period of time. Parameters developed represent limits which, if exceeded, must be dealt with in one fashion or another.

Establishing the Master Plan

A master production plan at the outset includes a forecast, actual orders and what remains as available to promise. ATP, or "Available To Promise," is the difference between the total demand and the actual customer orders that have been booked into a particular planning period. If ATP is a positive quantity, marketing can still commit the positive quantity of products to customers to be delivered in that period of the master production plan. By definition, ATP inside the demand time fence is always zero. Outside the demand time fence, ATP is the total demand minus the actual customer orders that have been committed. Whether these are actual customer orders or committed orders by marketing via finished goods replenishment is not relevant to manufacturing. The ATP figure serves marketing and customer service as a guide as to when they can promise product. Marketing or customer service cannot commit a customer order either inside the demand time fence or in a period when ATP is zero or less. Initially, the forecast itself determines the production plan, then a blend of forecast and actual orders, then actual customer and finished goods replenishment orders alone. Marketing either gets sufficient orders from customers, cuts forecasts to actual orders, or issues an order of replenishment to finished goods inventory. After the smoke of the initial forecast has cleared, the grace period ends, and the reality of what has transpired to date takes control. Material inventory may be delivered based upon the total demand and, therefore, needs to be meticulously managed within the acceptable control limits.

Time Fences

A demand time fence allows for no changes or deviations whatsoever. Production rates are fixed for a short period of time, at least as long as the total product cycle time. Within the demand time fence, the production plan will not be changed. Therefore, if there is currently a negotiated production plan of 100 units per day, then, within the demand time fence, production will be limited to precisely 100 units per day—no more, no less. As the total product cycle time is reduced, marketing will be allowed to make changes in a shorter period. The shortening of the total product cycle time helps achieve a key element in the manufacturing process: flexibility. Controlled flexibility is the primary objective. As an example, if total product cycle time for a particular product is three days, the daily rate will not be changed within this three-day period because the demand time fence is after the third day. Therefore, producing 100 units per day with the demand time fence on the third day, 100 units will be produced each of the three days. If total product cycle time can be reduced to two days, the demand time fence can be moved in from the third day to the second day. Demand time fence and planning flex fence techniques are always applied against the total demand quantity that has been previously computed. If the forecast had been greater than the actual customer orders, and if, in anticipation of orders, marketing wanted the forecast quantity produced, then it could issue a finished goods replenishment order outside the demand time fence. Outside the demand time fence, marketing will be allowed to make changes to the total demand. After the short, fixed period, a longer, gradually increasing and more flexible period will follow.

Planning Flex Fence

This flexible period, which gives marketing substantially greater flexibility in responding to customer demand, is associated with the planning flex fence. It is critical that planning flex fences negotiated with marketing be synchronized with the capabilities of the production process and with the suppliers. Planning flex fences allow plus and minus percentage changes to total demand within a particular time period. Typically the recommended number and magnitude of flex fences is three; as an example:

1. 5 percent flexibility within two weeks

2. 15 percent flexibility within four weeks

3. 30 percent flexibility within six weeks

Since the Demand Flow production process is designed at the highest targeted capacity in order to meet market fluctuations, it is reasonable to achieve a 20 to 30 percent increase in production plan by working additional hours and without requiring a line design change (reference Figure 4-3). Typically the greatest planning flex fence should not exceed the highest rate that the production process has been set up to produce. Any greater change beyond this capacity may require a major redesign of the production process and the addition of more people or machines to the process.

Flexibility Level/Limit Provided

The combined use of these types of fences provide both a level and limit of flexibility over time. The level and limit are achieved through a negotiated balance of the three factors:

1. Marketing requirements

2. Suppliers' capability

3. Total product cycle time

The necessary flexibility from suppliers must be reflected in contracts that are signed with those flow suppliers. The necessary conversation, coordination and negotiation between marketing and production is maintained by a minimum of weekly planning meetings between the two. Led by marketing's sales tracking, the two departments work to avoid spikes and to moderate both increasing and decreasing sales trends. The objective is to follow the customer demand directly and to deal with substantially increased or decreased sales without creating production line upheavals. Elementary to the success of the planning is that marketing violations of its forecast must be tracked, reported and negotiated; the negotiated flexibility among the three factors must be consistent, and product linearity must be achieved.

Demand Flow Materials Management

Once the total demand has been calculated, the flexible percentage in each time fence is applied against the total demand period by period. The changes are not cumulative changes but are always against the negotiated volume of the product. The master production planning process should be verified in a simulation mode. Violations that have been reported are negotiated, and the master production plan is always updated. This requires that the formal computer planning system must have a simulation mode that allows for calculating total demand and applying flex fence percentages against them, without driving down to the parts level and giving purchasing requirements to buy material against a plan that has not been approved.

During the internal negotiations, it should be noted that the key week in the production planning process is the first week outside the demand time fence. Once the move has been made inside the demand time fence, the production plan is fixed and the agreed-upon plan is executed. While in the first week

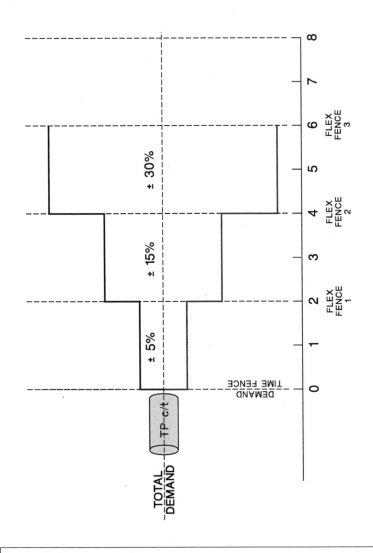

Figure 4-3 Demand and Planning Flexible Windows

outside the demand time fence, marketing and manufacturing must agree on the plan that moves into the demand time fence. At that point, two things can happen:

1. The total demand must be changed to match the negotiated level, or

2. A new level must be negotiated.

If a new level is negotiated, then demand and planning flex fence percentages will be applied against the new level for all periods of the planning horizon.

Flexibility Gains Market Share

Using the time fences and following negotiations between suppliers, marketing and the production process, a likely scenario for the flow of materials at the outset would be as follows: Production would manufacture 100 units per day for the first week, a period sufficient to cover total product cycle time. Supplier parts sufficient for that production volume would be available. There would be no deviation through this initial period in the total product cycle time. For the following two weeks there would be a flexibility of plus or minus five percent. Marketing could order anywhere between 95 and 105 units per day, but no more or no less. Then, in a later flex fence, perhaps four or eight weeks later, the flexibility would increase to 15 percent and, after a similar period, it would reach 30 percent. At that point, marketing could order anywhere between 70 and 130 units per day, but no more or no less. The gradually growing range of flexibility coordinates and takes into account manufacturing and supplier capabilities with marketing's demands. Suppliers must have a contract with similar flex ranges negotiated into their flexible contract, or inventory must be carried for long lead time items in order to meet flex requirements for noncontracted items.

Developing Master Plan

There are eight basic steps to developing the master production plan which evolves largely through weekly negotiations between marketing, production, and production planning.

- The eight-step process begins with receipt of a forecast and actual orders from marketing.

- The total demand will be determined, period by period, using the forecast and actual orders that have been received via forecast consumption techniques.

- Once the total demand has been determined, demand and planning flex fence percentages are applied against the total demand. Any violations are reported to marketing which is requested to make appropriate changes to the forecast or actual orders depending on where the violations occurred.

- Once marketing has made the appropriate changes, the master production plan can again be calculated to arrive at a total demand that is without violation. Initially, many violations are to be expected; but once the process is further understood and changes made, the number of violations should diminish.

* Once an acceptable forecast has been received, a production plan will be developed.

* Then, another check will be made to ensure that the production plan can be supported by production capacity. An undercapacity schedule of about 85 to 92 percent is preferred to avoid compromising quality, to always make the daily rate, and to allow for the necessary training.

* The plan can then be broken down into a daily rate using a manufacturing calendar which will provide the number of work days in a week, holidays and so forth.

* The final step is to consider product options which will be built and which will determine the mixed-model sequencing.

Negotiating Violations

Some violations which exceed the outer limits of the flex fences can be eliminated by moving goods to customers or to finished goods inventory. Marketing may call a customer and ask that an order be taken a week early or, to ease the opposite problem in some cases, a week late.

The process moves from an "initial" forecast to a "negotiated" forecast. The shifting in time of actual orders with customer cooperation and movement of products to finished goods inventory represents an important tool used by marketing in achieving compliance. This is another reason marketing is asked to become the "owner" of finished goods inventory.

Production Plan/Capacity Check

The production plan is then developed, leveling the peaks and valleys with linearity as a primary objective. This is where a few weeks of 120 units and a few weeks of 110 units are all made 115, and a double check is made to ensure the volume is acceptable and doable. A further check involves analyzing the volume against planned capacity to come up with a percentage of capacity. A production plan running 80 to 89 percent of planned capacity would be desirable (refer to figure 4-4). The development of a production plan that is different from a negotiated total demand is an optional and cautious step. It must be agreed that the plan can be supported by manufacturing. If acceptable to marketing, the peaks and valleys can be leveled. This cannot always be done, especially in cases where it may negatively impact the customers. This "smoothing" process allows better linearity and consistent production operations.

Daily Rate/Mixed-Model Sequencing

With five work days per week, the 115-unit weekly production plan becomes a daily rate of 23. At this point, a check of required options is made to see if machines, people and cycle times are sufficiently similar so that the different option units

PRODUCTION PLAN

	WEEK 1	WEEK 2	WEEK 3	WEEK 4	WEEK 5	WEEK 6	WEEK 7	WEEK 8
FORECAST :								
ACTUAL ORDERS :								
TOTAL DEMAND :	110	110	120	110	100	125	130	100
PRODUCTION PLAN :	110	110	115	115	110	115	120	110

PRODUCTION PLAN AGAINST CAPACITY

	WEEK 1	WEEK 2	WEEK 3	WEEK 4	WEEK 5	WEEK 6	WEEK 7	WEEK 8
FORECAST :								
ACTUAL ORDERS :								
TOTAL DEMAND :								
PRODUCTION PLAN :	110	110	115	115	110	115	120	110
CAPACITY :	130	130	130	130	130	130	130	130
% CAPACITY :	85	85	88	85	85	88	92	85

Figure 4-4 Demand-Based Plan

can be run on the same line or cell by utilizing group technology techniques. When different options or models use the same machines and people, mixed-model sequencing production should be considered as a means of smoothing the flow and the work content between products. Mixed-model sequencing is also desired to minimize exposure to quality problems because fewer numbers of a particular model will be built at one time. In addition, the line will produce a lower cost product with a higher continual focus on quality by using the predictable mixed-model sequence, or repeatable sequence coming on a regular basis. Also, imbalances in work content among options on a line will not be as disruptive, plus marketing can actually promise a mix of orders within a day. As an example, if the weekly demand was for 77 units of the standard model, 25 with option A, 10 with option B, and 3 with option C, the mixed-Model sequenced plan might include 15 standard units, 5 with option A, 2 with option B, and 1 with option C. On the second day, the plan would be the same except option C would be omitted. The first- and second-day plans would alternate every other day. Under such a plan, the units would not be in a batch, but would be mixed throughout the day.

Why Linearity?

In traditional scheduled manufacturing, the primary objective is to meet the monthly goal regardless of when it is met in the month. Some traditional production charts look like hockey sticks with little production through the month until the last few days when virtually all production takes place. Others sag—

they start out near what would be an average daily rate, and end up that way, but drop off substantially for several days between.

Demand Flow manufacturing emphasizes linearity for several reasons. Wide variations in the daily rate usually mean that overtime will be needed to catch up. The overtime needed to catch up is a combination of additional overhead and usually a time-and-a-half cost of labor. A wide variation in daily production generally causes or aggravates quality problems. Finished goods analyses consistently reveal that units produced at the end of a hectic production month have nearly twice the defect rate as units produced at normal times of the month.

The consistency of production tends to promote consistency of quality. That consistency also raises customer satisfaction and service levels. Marketing can promise an order to a customer on a specific day and have reasonable expectations that the unit will be produced at that date, rather than a vague promise of sometime in the month. Also, the short-term focus of a daily rate eases performance monitoring and makes goals more attainable. The shorter the term of the goal, the more likely it is to be met. Linearity is substantially more cost efficient. It produces higher quality, higher customer satisfaction and service, and is a more attainable goal for production.

Measuring Linearity

Performance against the master production plan should be measured on a daily basis. Actual production compared against the planned daily production rate will yield deviations. Deviations should be tracked on the basis of: deviation for the day, sum of the absolute deviations for the month to date, net deviations, and the cause of deviations. There is no comfort to be taken in offsetting deviations so that, at the end of the month, the net deviations column stands at zero.

As an example, consider a nine-day period in which the production rate is four per day and the actual production volumes are as follows: 3, 4, 5, 3, 4, 5, 3, 4, 5. The production rate and actual rate both total 36. Traditionally, the net deviation totals zero because the overproduction and underproduction canceled out. Yet, the sum of the absolute deviations is six. The sum of the absolute deviations, a cumulative figure that can only increase, serves as the basis for calculating the linearity index.

Formula for linearity index is:

$$Linearity\ Index\ \% \ = \ \left(1 - \left[\frac{Sum\ of\ Absolute\ Deviations}{Total\ Rate}\right]\right) x\ 100$$

In the example above, the linearity index formula would be: 1 minus [6 divided by 36] times 100 percent, for a linearity index of 83.3 percent. Flow manufacturers should not seek daily delivery of supplies until a linearity index of at least 90 percent is achieved. Each cause of deviation should be listed and analyzed—the objective is to eliminate such causes and achieve greater linearity.

In summary, the goal of the *world-class* manufacturer is to be a Demand-Based producer in a flexible Demand Flow process. Total quality products are built in a linear flow equal to the targeted daily rate. It is a major goal to achieve adherence to customer demand. Flexible time fence and planning flex fence controls are essential in order to allow marketing to make the necessary small changes in a short period of time and eliminate the large spikes prevalent in traditional scheduled manufacturing. The likely results: high customer satisfaction and service levels with a minimum of inventory investment and a flexible, cost-effective Demand Flow Technology production process.

Chapter Five

Kanban Pull and Backflush Techniques

In Western countries, the philosophy that pulls material upon demand is called Just-In-Time inventory. In Japan, it is often referred to as Kanban Manufacturing. Kanban is a very powerful technique that is more than a tool that executes the pull philosophy. It is more than the Japanese-to-English translation of "communication signal" or "card." Kanban is the primary tow chain in a demand pull system; it is the replacement of reams of paper associated with scheduling and issue actions. It is frequently a key to the savings of many millions of dollars per year because of the substantial reduction in time that materials are carried in inventory as compared with traditional schedulized manufacturing. Demand Flow Technology (DFT) moves away from the issue and scheduling philosophy of manufacturing to the Kanban demand pull philosophy where the material is pulled to the point, and at the time it is needed—no sooner.

Raw-In-Process Inventory

In Demand Flow manufacturing, there are points of replenishment (resupply), inventory supply areas, carts or stations close to the consuming line or feeder processes that they serve. It should be emphasized that these supply areas stock material at or near where it will be consumed. When components or materials are needed on the consuming line, they are pulled from these point-of-replenishment supply areas. These supply areas in turn pull from a storeroom, while one still remains at the plant, but *ultimately,* these supply areas will be replenished by a pull directly from an external supplier. Between the point-of-replenishment supply area and the consuming line, there is never a computer transaction—parts should never be counted between those points. From the standpoint of inventory management and cost accounting, the line and the point-of-replenishment supply areas are all in "Raw and in-process" (RIP) inventory. All of the materials and parts, whether they are on the line or at various supply points, are considered to be in RIP. Materials kept in a storeroom, whether it be traditional or Demand Flow manufacturing, are still classified as raw material. A physical count and a computer account transfer should be required to move inventory from a storeroom (RAW) into RIP (reference Figure 5-1).

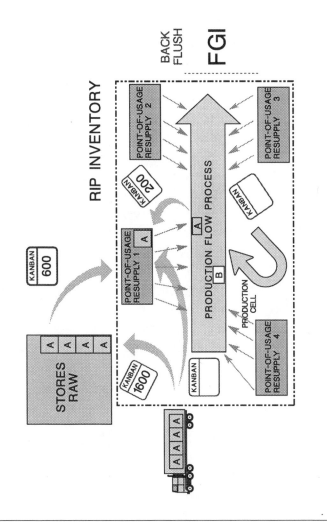

Figure 5-1 Raw and In-Process Inventory

RIP Inclusive

For purposes of inventory, RIP excludes all storeroom (RAW) materials and considers anything from completion of the product back to the point where supplies first enter the process as RIP. Material is pulled into the process, either from a storeroom or the supplier. What comes into RIP from suppliers or the storeroom is the subject of a computer transaction. A receipt transaction serves as an acknowledgment of a specific quantity of materials from the supplier into RIP or from the supplier into the storeroom. However, the movement of material from any RIP point to any other point in the process is not tracked. Everything in the point-of-replenishment supply areas and on the line is considered RIP inventory. As a rule of thumb, at this point there are approximately five days of raw parts in RIP. This rule starts from the very first day that the flow process is designed and started. In Demand Flow manufacturing the exact location of material within that RIP area is known, but since the quantity is so small, the exact quantity at each location is not a topic of concern—what is known is the exact total inventory count in RIP in aggregate at any given time. In Demand Flow manufacturing there should not be any counting or computer transaction between the point-of-replenishment supply areas and the consuming line.

Backflushing for Relieving RIP Inventory

Once the completed product is passed from production to finished goods inventory to become available for shipment, the product bill of material is backflushed to relieve the component parts from the RIP inventory. This backflushing technique is a computer and financial transaction. It is the gate through which product completion and material consumption is measured with a minimum of counting and paperwork. A backflush transaction must occur when completed products go into finished goods inventory. Once a standard bicycle, as an example, reaches finished goods, backflushing will automatically take from inventory the bicycle's bill of material, i.e., two tires, one handlebar, one seat, so many spokes, and so forth.

Since inventory in RIP is considered as one large bucket with approximately a week's worth of inventory parts and dollars, it is not a practical matter to actively cycle count in the flow process. What is in RIP is auditable, but it should not be cycle counted on a routine basis. If accounting feels the need to audit inventory in RIP, they can go out and audit the material in RIP. This includes all material in the process prior to backflush, whether it is in the point-of-replenishment supply area, in a line Kanban, or partially completed. Although a flow production process can be audited, it should not be actively cycle counted as in traditional scheduled manufacturing.

Eventual Elimination of Stores

Although an important goal of Demand Flow manufacturing is to eliminate the central storeroom, this does *not* mean that you should take apart your central storeroom and scatter the remaining inventory throughout the product area. This goal can only be reached once the combined Raw and RIP inventory turns have reached 50 per year. Inventory turnover calculations refer to the total annual inventory investment for a part, divided by the average total amount of inventory for the part in all areas:

- Line

- RIP

- Finished goods

- Stores

If the total annual material cost for one particular product is equal to $1 million, and if there is currently an on-hand inventory of $100,000 of the parts to produce the product, then the inventory turnover for that product is ten per year. With an inventory turnover of ten, a storeroom will be needed to store material. Approximately a week's worth of purchased materials can be held in RIP; more than a week's worth of most material would require a storeroom. In the example above, 1/50, or approximately $20,000, of that material will be kept in RIP; the additional $80,000 will be kept in the storeroom. If $20,000 became sufficient for the total inventory on-hand, the part would no longer require a storeroom and the material would be pulled directly from the supplier into the point-of-replenishment supply area rather than from the storeroom.

Quality problems, delivery problems, and the fact that suppliers may not yet have been placed under a DFT contract are additional reasons for maintaining a storeroom. Since the Demand Flow process does not produce subassemblies or pick kits of parts, as is the case in traditional manufacturing, the central storeroom function of picking parts based upon a pre-determined schedule is eliminated. RIP will contain only approximately a week's supply of parts, and the balance of parts will remain in the storeroom. RIP requires a degree of trust in employees in managing the flow process. Some half-measure DFT practitioners have dangerously claimed compliance with that objective by simply taking down the old sign over the storeroom and replacing it with a *faddish* one that says "RIP."

Extremely Hazardous

Conversely, some suicidal practitioners have not only eliminated the storeroom, but they do not use point-of-replenishment supply areas—they take supplies directly from the trucks to the consuming lines, which can be as dangerous as the sign relocation practice. The direct supplier-to-line connection must be based on substantial trust, a total quality part, prepackaged parts, 100 percent on-time delivery, 100 percent supplier certification, and a flow production process of 100 percent yield. Although this can be achieved, it is initially preferred to deliver to the point of replenishment in RIP and to pull from there directly to the consuming line. Eventually with a TQC part, TQC supplier, and TQC process, the part will be delivered directly from the supplier to the consuming line.

Kanban Techniques

Kanban is a technique that is used to signal a replenishment. The Kanban, though basically a uniform card, can take several different shapes and functions as well. The Kanban signal can be a card, container-based electronic communication, or a combination of multiple cards. When the Kanban card is attached to a container, the container with the card attached is referred to as a Kanban container. The basic Kanban is a card that shows point of usage (where the part is consumed), point of supply (the point from which the part is replenished), quantity, and part number and description.

The complete information on the Kanban card makes it an effective replenishment tool because it specifically describes where material comes from and where it is consumed. Except for the affected pull quantity, Kanban information is very specific. If we reference Figure 5-2, the Kanban card has the following information on it: Part Number 110407-01; Description, Resistor, 32 ohms, 1/4 watt, 5 percent; Usage, Cell - 4-3; Supply, RIP - P; Pull Quantity, fill to line. That means simply that Cell 4-3 is consuming that particular resistor and it is replenished from RIP - P. The quantity of parts that are pulled when the container is emptied is based upon an approximate quantity in a particular container filled to a line marked inside the container.

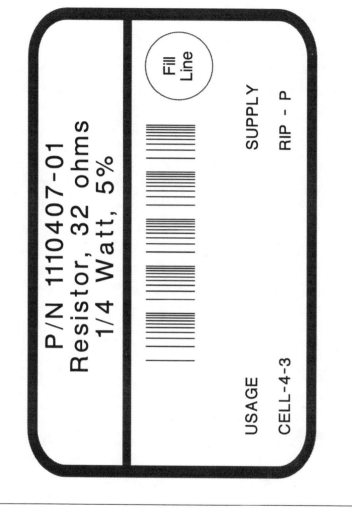

Figure 5-2 Kanban Signal

Signal for Replenishment

Kanban is a technique of the Demand Flow manufacturing material replenishment system. Using a single-card/container Kanban technique, when a Kanban container is emptied it is to be refilled. It is replenished from the point of supply listed on the Kanban card. The quantity indicated is pulled back from the point of supply to the point of consumption listed on the Kanban. The Kanban pull process is defined as the points of supply and usage of a particular part. Thus, all of the information required to replenish Kanbans is listed on the card.

A material handler is usually employed to "roam the production process" and replenish raw material Kanbans. The average amount of time required to make a "milk run" of the process and replenish Kanbans is known as replenishment time. This time is a key ingredient in Kanban sizing.

Kanban is not tied to a specific product kit or work order—it is tied to specific points of usage and supply. Multiple products built on the same line would use the same component part number that was pulled by a common Kanban container. Kanban cards should not be identified to the specific product that uses this particular part.

Kanban Pull Sequences

There can be many different Kanban pull sequences which are expressed in terms of points of usage and supply. In addition to Kanbans between points on the line and the point-of-replenishment supply area, Kanbans are also used to pull material between RIP and storeroom, RIP and supplier, and supplier and storeroom. Kanbans travel back and forth from point of usage to point of supply as needed. The Kanban returns with the identified materials pulled.

In-Process Kanban

Kanban is also used whenever there is an imbalance between two consecutive operations in the flow process. The in-process Kanban does not have a part number identity. It can be as simple as a square with a large "X" on it. An in-process Kanban between operators is used to alleviate an imbalance in the line. Thus, there is a difference between the common material Kanban, which is used to pull material, and an in-process Kanban, which is, in effect, a buildup of units to allow an imbalanced operation to work additional hours of overtime or an additional work shift.

Kanban Pull Quantities

Counting or verifying a quantity of parts between the supplier and storeroom, between the supplier and RIP, or between the storeroom and RIP is essential. However, since there are no inventory transactions within the RIP area, there is no need to count specific quantities of parts within that area. Furthermore, since there is no value in counting parts—there is every reason to avoid counting parts on the line. Pulls from the point-of-replenishment supply areas in RIP to the line should be as quick and efficient as possible. Thus, the preferred "quantity" shown on the line Kanban would be the prepackaged quantity, e.g., one box, or one pallet, or two packages, one case, three rolls, or an easily measured quantity such as a tablespoonful, replenish to a measured point, fill up to a marked line, and so forth. Minimum/maximum quantities should *never* appear on a Kanban and should also be avoided. Minimum/maximum techniques of traditional manufacturing have no place in the efficient Kanban pull system. They require more detailed measurement, and they continually require counting and re-counting.

Kanbans that are pulled from a supplier would include a specific pull quantity. It is acceptable to pull the Kanban quantity or less—never more. Depending on part usage, physical size, supplier quality, delivery and other factors, the quantity pulled to the line with a Kanban may represent several days, one day, or just a few hours of usage. Where possible, reusable containers should be used as the Kanban itself and serve several purposes. Such containers, filled as identified by the attached Kanban card, in addition to serving as the Kanban, would simplify quantity determinations, reduce supplier packaging costs, and reduce packaging waste in the plant.

Single-Card Kanban/Container Techniques

Using a single-card/container technique, the consumption of a container of parts will trigger a replenishment of the Kanban quantity of that part. When the production operators empty the first container of parts, they would place the empty container in a properly identified area beside them. They would immediately pull a second full container of the same part, that was originally behind the first container, and continue to build the product. The material handlers that "roam" the RIP areas replenishing Kanbans would take the empty container and read the attached Kanban information. They would go to the identified point of replenishment (supply area) and fill the container with the quantity of parts identified on the Kanban. They would return the filled container back to the consumption point and place it behind the container currently being used by the production operator. If each container had $1\frac{1}{2}$ to $2\frac{1}{2}$ days of parts in it, the material handlers would have that time ($1\frac{1}{2}$ to $2\frac{1}{2}$ days) to replenish the container of parts.

This is an example of the single-card/container technique using two containers of parts. Additional containers, e.g., two, three, four or more, could be used employing the single-card/container technique. When each is consumed, it is replenished. The only time a single-card/container technique, which uses only one container, can be effectively used is when the production operator is responsible for replenishing the material. In such cases, the material replenishment time should be added to the TQC sequence of events to produce the product.

Dual- and Multiple-Card Techniques

Using a dual-card Kanban technique when a container of parts is pulled may not trigger an immediate replenishment of that part. The dual-card technique uses a move Kanban and a produce Kanban card. The move card is used to pull a quantity of material from a point of supply back to the consuming process. The produce card is used to identify the replenishment quantity of parts that will again be produced to satisfy the consuming demand. Material is being pulled in one (move) quantity and being replenished in another (produce) quantity.

The dual-card technique is commonly found in machine cells where the process time is very lengthy or where yield or setup issues prevent a machine from producing in the much smaller move quantities. As an example, let's take a machine cell, XE, that produces several different parts for various consuming flow lines (reference Figure 5-3). Because of a lengthy heat-treat operation in this cell, parts cannot be produced in quantities that are less than 100 pieces. Parts that are manufactured in this cell are taken to a point-of-replenishment supply area, RIP-C1. Several different flow lines pull part number 10063 that is produced in cell XE from the same supply area, RIP-C1. When part 10063 is manufactured, four containers of 25 are produced and taken to RIP-C1. Each of the containers has a produce Kanban attached. Each produce Kanban card has a quantity of 25, and it has a "1 of 4" notation on each produce Kanban card (reference Figure 5-4).

When the part 10063 is consumed in the flow lines, the material handlers would read the move Kanban card and go to RIP-C1 and pull a container of part 10063 back to the consuming line. When the part is pulled from the RIP-C1 supply area, they would remove the produce Kanban card from the container of parts and place the produce card in a collection box. Through-

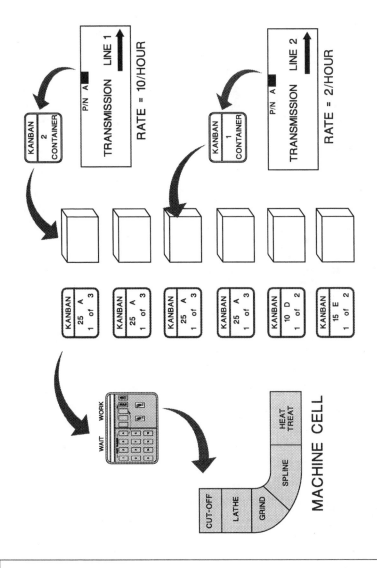

Figure 5-3 Dual-Card Technique

Figure 5-4 Produce Kanban

out the day the produce cards are removed from the collection box and taken back to cell XE. When the cell XE gets "four" produce cards, production would begin on another 100 of part 10063. The parts are being moved in containers of 25 and replenished in quantities of 100. It is very likely that there would be at least five Kanban produce cards each with the same "1 of 4" notation on them. This would allow a container of 25 to remain in-process while additional parts are being manufactured.

Kanban Sizing

Kanban size is calculated initially when the process is designed. The process is designed at capacity, which is the highest required rate, with the Kanban sizing calculated accordingly. The quantity developed through the Kanban sizing formula will be the minimum amount of material in the process to support this rate. Less than the minimum will result in shortages in the production process before the Kanban can be replenished. The formula is used for all line, RIP and supplier-to-stores Kanbans as well. Once the size of Kanban has been established, it is preferable to make adjustments by increasing or reducing replenishment time. Unless there is a permanent and dramatic change in demand, it is preferable not to resize Kanbans. To calculate Kanban size, divide the result of the total demand of each product per shift (D) multiplied by the usage quantity per product bill of material (Q) multiplied by replenishment time (R). To express replenishment time in hours, R should be divided by the number of hours in a shift (H). To use a prepackaged container quantity for a Kanban quantity, divide that demand quantity by work hours per shift (H) multiplied by supplier package quantity (P):

$$Kanban\ Size\ =\ \frac{\Sigma\,(D\,x\,Q)\,R}{H\,x\,P}$$

D   =   Daily Rate Per Product Per Shift

Q   =   Usage Quantity Per Product

R   =   Replenishment Time (Hrs.)

H   =   Work Hours Per Shift

P   =   Supplier Package Quantity (if applicable)

Consider a part with the following: total demand, 120 units; usage quantity per unit, 17; replenishment time, 2 hours; work hours per shift, 7.5; supplier packaging, 25 per package. The minimum Kanban quantity would be 120 times 17 times 2 divided by 7.5 times 25, or 22 packages, which would be 550 pieces. If there is yield loss on a component, it should be factored in the usage quantity.

The total demand of a part should be used for Kanban sizing. As an example, three products are built on a mixed-model flow line. Product X has a total demand of 50 per day. Product Y has a total demand of 40 per day. Product Z has a total demand of five per day. Each product uses one component part W at the same consuming location on the line. The minimum size of the line Kanban in part W would be given a replenishment time of four hours and would be sized as follows:

$$50 \ x \ 1 = 50$$
$$40 \ x \ 1 = 40$$
$$\underline{5 \ x \ 1 = \ \ 5}$$
$$95$$

$$Total \ Demand = \frac{95 \ x \ 4}{7.5} = 51 \ pieces$$

If there are approximately 60 part Ws per measured cup, the line Kanban would contain a pull quantity of one cup. Unless there is a special need to precisely count part W, the visual count quantity will be used between the line and the RIP supply point.

When a new product is added to the process and it does not significantly increase the total rate per shift or the total usage quantity of the material already in the process, there would be no need to add to existing Kanbans or change the size of the Kanbans. However, if new material requirements or a significant change in the total daily rate per shift or usage quantity occurs, existing Kanbans may be increased or multiple Kanbans may be added.

Backflushing the Bill of Material

The Demand Flow manufacturing bill of material is also used for effective inventory control on parts in RIP. A computer technique referred to as backflush is used to relieve the component on-hand inventory from RIP for the component parts that were used to build a product. The computer backflush transaction is performed when the final product is completed. The product bill of material is deducted from the on-hand RIP inventory by the computer backflush transaction. The basic premise of the backflush technique is that if the product was built, the bill of material for the product must have been used.

In order to perform a backflush transaction, there is some additional information on the DFT bill of material that is typically not on the traditional product bill of material.

Backflush Information

The bill of material for a product will not only include the component part numbers and quantity per unit but also the backflush location and deduct identification as well. The back-flush location will identify where the component part is to be deducted from when the product bill of material is backflushed. The backflush location for products produced in a single facility is usually identified as "RIP." The component part number and its associated "quantity per" would be relieved from on-hand quantity at the backflush location shown (reference Figure 5-5). It is possible that the inventory from the DFT bill of material could be consumed at different backflush locations. If such instances occur, the product bill of material would show a component part number listed twice with different quantities and different backflush locations. This would be the case if a manufacturer had two different production buildings and if some of the parts were consumed and backflushed from build-ing one RIP, while others were consumed and backflushed from building two RIP. Products built on multiple lines may have

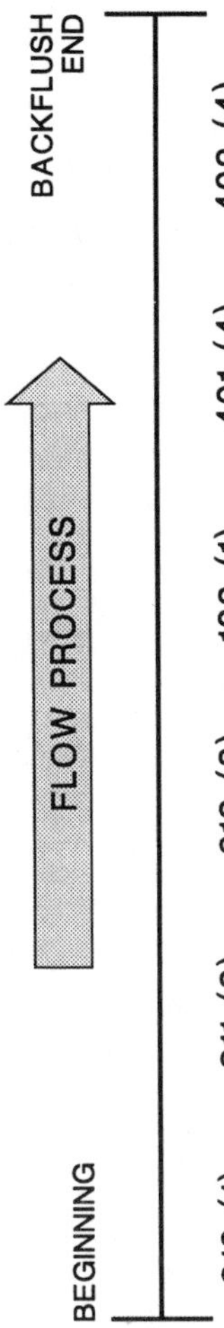

BEGINNING → FLOW PROCESS → BACKFLUSH END

210 (1) 211 (8) 212 (8) 103 (1) 401 (4) 402 (4)

PART NUMBER	QUANTITY ON-HAND BEFORE/AFTER BACKFLUSH	LOCATION	IN-PROCESS
210	12 / 11	RIP	0
211	63 / 55	RIP	0
212	44 / 36	RIP	0
103	9 / 8	RIP	0
401	12 / 8	RIP	0
402	9 / 5	RIP	0

Figure 5-5 Backflush Techniques

separate and distinct backflush locations, although in all cases there would be only one product bill of material. In that case, a line identification number would be tied to a product to define the backflush location for the product being produced. So when the backflush transaction is conducted on a computer, it will specify the product part number and the line identification. The computer system would get the appropriate backflush location based upon that information.

Bill of Materials (BOM) Planned Usage

The key point on backflush is planned usage—if the product was built, the product bill of material was consumed. This requires a high degree of accuracy in the bill of material as well as the requirement that any part that is to be controlled in inventory must be on the bill of material. Thus, packaging and other traditional expense items, to the extent possible, should be put on the bill of material. If the usage of a component can be consistently predicted, then it should be on the bill of material. Traditional techniques such as order point and minimum/maximum systems should be eliminated—the bill of material should be the primary control if usage can be predicted. The DFT bill of material must be accurate and complete, and it may also be more detailed than the traditional bill of material.

Backflush at a Deduct Point

The concept of an intermediate computer backflush transaction is to take a portion of the product bill of material and relieve only those parts from the RIP inventory prior to completion of the final product. An intermediate backflush is performed at a *physical location* in the production process known as a deduct point. When an intermediate backflush is performed, the parts relieved from the RIP inventory are placed in a special holding bucket called "in-process backflush inventory." When a component part has been placed in the in-process backflush inventory, that means that its bill of material quantity has been relieved from RIP, but these component parts have not yet reached the end of the process as a part of the final completed product. At the time of an intermediate backflush, those parts consumed up to the physical deduct point are relieved from the backflush location of the flow manufacturing bill of material and placed into an in-process backflush inventory.

Final Backflush Follows Intermediate

When the product is completed and placed into finished goods, a final backflush is done against the entire product bill of material. The portion of the product that is in the in-process backflush inventory will be taken from that in-process inventory "bucket" and the portion of the components on the bill of material that had not yet been relieved at the intermediate deduct point will then be taken from the backflush location. The rule for this computer transaction is simple: if the component part quantity is in the in-process inventory "bucket," take it from this in-process inventory; if it is not on hand in in-process, relieve the inventory from the appropriate backflush locations. This way, the total on-hand inventory balance from a formal computer system standpoint can never be misstated. It cannot be assumed that the inventory consumed at the intermediate deduct point is no longer on hand in RIP. That would cause the purchasing planning system to assume those component parts were used and create an immediate replenishment for those component parts. From the standpoint of the formal computer system, these parts are still considered as on-hand inventory; they are simply in an in-process holding inventory "bucket" waiting for the final backflush of the completed product.

Not a Mandatory Transaction

It is not essential to have any intermediate backflush or deduct point in the flow production process. However, sometimes such points may be desirable. Sometimes, in very lengthy processes where the total product cycle time exceeds three days, the intermediate backflush may be necessary to assist in managing inventory control. Under these and certain other circumstances, an intermediate backflush or deduct point may be quite advantageous. As an example, if 95 percent of the parts are consumed prior to a lengthy burn-in operation, perhaps ten days, an intermediate backflush of the 95 percent would do two things:

1. It would allow an audit of the component parts up to the burn-in operation without having to count parts in the burn-in operation.

2. Also, it would allow any nonrepairable failures from the burn-in process to be backflushed to scrap as a single entity rather than as several independent parts.

In this example, the balance, or remaining five percent of component parts consumed after the burn-in operation, would be backflushed as usual at finished goods.

Intermediate deduct points should not be used without good reason. They are not recommended unless there is a scenario similar to the example outlined. While intermediate deduct or intermediate backflush points are not necessary, lengthy processes tend to have at least one for effective inventory control and auditing purposes.

Scrap

Scrap is one of the items handled in Demand Flow manufacturing in a very different way than it is handled in traditional scheduled manufacturing. Visual techniques are used and the paperwork is handled by the material handlers—operators are kept free of the scrap paperwork morass. A preferred method of keeping the operators free of paperwork involves the use of a poker chip. When operators find a bad part, they place a poker chip in their line Kanban. Each poker chip in the Kanban would represent one piece of defective material. When material handlers replenish that empty Kanban, they would note the number of poker chips and write the appropriate scrap tickets. Since the backflush transaction will deduct only the planned consumption of a component part, any unplanned consumption, such as extra usage or scrap, must be reported.

The scrap transactions are reported against parts. In the case of a nonrepairable final product, all of the consumed component parts can be backflushed from RIP inventory into a scrap account for the final product. In Demand Flow manufacturing, scrap must be handled separately—it is not a part of the planned backflush. Scrap must be done outside the backflush transaction of the DFT bill of material. Extreme caution should be used in predicting yield on a particular component part. If the yield is above or below the prediction, then the on-hand inventory will be misstated. Failure to report scrap in a timely fashion will make it impossible to have correct inventory balances.

In scrap transactions, only the material value of the component or the assembly that has been scrapped will be applied. There should be no partial labor or overhead credit due to a partially assembled unit or to a portion of the production process being completed. Transactions should be made only against the material portion of the component or assembly.

Communication to Pull

Kanban is the method of getting material into the flow production process, compared to the work order issues and scheduling of traditional manufacturing. It is a communication technique that tells where to get the material, where to take it, and when to pull the material. Kanban sizing is calculated at the minimum Kanban quantity necessary to support the designed product or mixed-model line rate. Although the volume of products produced can be continuously changed, the Kanban quantities are rarely affected or re-sized. Single-card or dual-card Kanban techniques are vital tools to the competitive *world-class* corporation.

Chapter Six

Group Technology and Machine Cells

Group technology is a technique in which dissimilar machines are grouped into single cells to produce families of similar-type products. The products that are produced within these cells will use the various machines or operations within the cell, but each product may require slightly more or less work time per machine or operation within the cell. Group technology is the organization of people and machines into cells to produce lower quantities of parts with reduced setups, reduced or eliminated queues, and reduced throughput times. Group technology also provides the opportunity to use flexible operators for multiple machines facilitating such efficiencies as an operator performing setup work on one machine while another machine is running. As an example, a machine cell of five different machines, depending upon the machine run time, would be run by one to five operators.

Machine Cells Give Flexibility

In scheduled manufacturing, machines are grouped into machine work centers according to function. Each of the similar individual machines within the functional work center is called a workstation. Products are then created by moving from functional work center to work center. As an example, a part that would require machine stamping, grinding and drilling would start off in the first work center performing the first operation, such as stamping. All parts would be stamped, and when the entire lot is stamped, then that lot would be sent over to the grinding work center. All parts would then be ground in the grinding work center and then transferred into the third work center for drilling.

In Demand Flow manufacturing, machine cells are set up consisting of dissimilar machines producing a family of products that requires the combination of various machine functions, such as stamping, grinding and drilling. The flow machine cell might include one stamping machine, one grinder and one drill rather than all of one functional type of machine, as is the case in the traditional work center. It is common to design a U-shaped machine arrangement in setting up a machine cell. The U-shape allows for operating a maximum number of machines in a relatively small area and enables one production employee to move easily from machine to machine with a minimal amount of move time within the cell (reference Figure 6-1).

When a product leaves a flow machine cell, it is complete in terms of the operations performed on it. In the example above, when it leaves the machine cell, the product is stamped, ground and drilled. To achieve the same degree in traditional manufacturing, the product would have been scheduled, queued, moved or routed to and through three completely different functional work centers.

Staffed by Flexible People

Multifunctional employees who work within the machine cell should be minimally capable of moving one-up and one-down through the various machines within the machine cell. A machine cell can consist of a single person or several people. Machine cells that are feeder cells should be arranged at or near their consuming production line. As machined parts are pulled into the consuming line, they are immediately verified and consumed. This provides greater communication and better quality control, and all parts produced are verified one at a time, not by the scheduled and inspected batch quantity. The multifunctional employees will move similar products smoothly through the cell. The group technology techniques to create machine cells in conjunction with the balancing techniques of the flow process will provide many opportunities in line designs. Cells are set up as close to the consuming line as

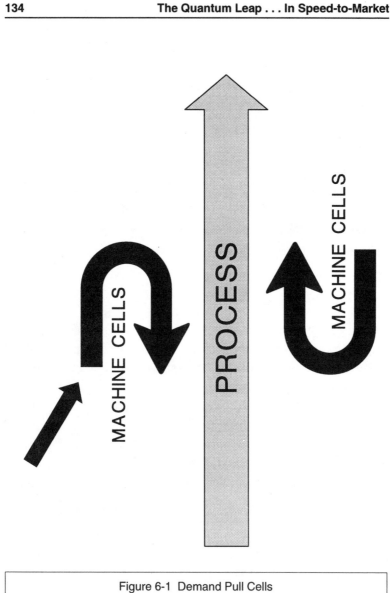

Figure 6-1 Demand Pull Cells

possible, and if a U-shaped layout is used, the cell will end near where it began as a result of that design and layout.

Demand Flow manufacturing machine cells tend to be considerably denser than the traditional work centers, and facility requirements, such as air conditioning, power, air pressure, lighting and environmental requirements, are just a few of the matters that must be considered in designing and locating a machine cell.

Mixed-Model Design

In achieving an efficient cell design for multiple product cells, process mapping techniques are employed to ascertain commonality of process and commonality of the product. The first step in setting up a mixed-model machine cell, or flow line, is to organize cells according to the various machines or operations required to produce a family of products. The products manufactured within a mixed-model machine cell or flow line should be common at the process level. The first step in identifying commonality at the process level is to create a product synchronization for each candidate product. The second step is to create a process map which contains the candidate product synchronizations (reference Figure 6-2). This will identify product commonality at the process level. Once the type of machines that will be required within the cell has been identified, the next objective is to identify those products that require the common processes within that cell. Process maps are cre-

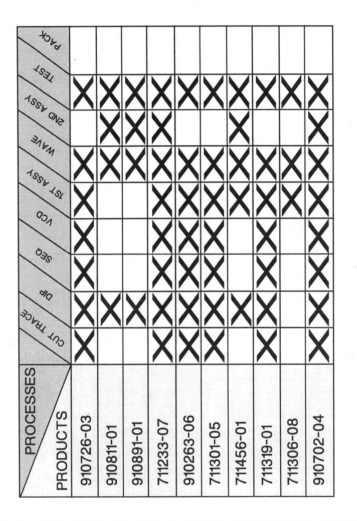

Figure 6-2 Process Map

ated to identify multiple products down one axis and machine processes or operations across the other.

Each product is reviewed to identify the particular processes or machine operations required to manufacture each product. The next step in cell design is to create a cell configuration that is made up of the common machines or operations identified in the process map. The physical cell layout will require those machines or operations for products that have the identified commonality, at the process level, within a machine cell or mixed-model flow line. Once the configuration of the machines or operations within a cell has been identified, then all of the products which are possible candidates—because they require those various machine processes—are identified.

Searching for Commonality

After identifying possible candidates for the machine cell or mixed-model flow line, each of these products that have commonality at the process level is broken into a TQC sequence of events. This identifies the work content and quality criteria for each of the products by operation or machine function within the machine cell or flow line. Once the work content time by machine function or operation is identified, the total time is calculated for all of the operations on the process map. This will identify the total time to produce each product that is a possible candidate based upon the common processes in the cell. The next objective is to group products that are, first, common in total time and, second, similar in the time required at each of the machine operations within the cell. Now another matrix will evolve identifying those similar products that require the common processes in this cell design. This matrix identifies the work content at each machine function or operation in the cell along with the total work content time of each product (reference Figure 6-3).

Using an operational and total time index, products with common processes and similar operational and total times are further isolated as final candidates for additional analysis.

Takt Time of a Cell

Targeted operational cycle time of a cell that is dedicated to a single part or product is established by multiplying the effective hours per shift by the number of shifts per day and dividing that by the designed daily rate (capacity) of the part or product to be run through the cell:

$$Cell\ Cycle\ Time = \frac{H(S)}{Dcp}$$

H   =   Effective Work Hours Per Shift

S   =   Shifts Per Day

Dcp =   Designed Daily Rate (Capacity)

In calculating the targeted operational cycle time of a mixed-model cell, the designed daily rate (capacity) is the sum of the individual rates of each of the similar products to be produced within the cell. This design Takt time is based upon

PRODUCTS	CUT TRACE	DIP	SEQ	VCD	1ST ASSY	WAVE	TEST	TOTAL
910726-03	5.2	15.2	9.1	6.2	17.4	1.7	8.5	63.3
910811-01	2.7	11.6	4.6	3.0	9.1	1.7	3.5	36.2
910891-01	5.0	11.2	5.1	3.9	7.6	1.7	3.5	38.0
711233-07	3.3	12.1	5.1	3.7	5.9	1.7	4.4	36.2
910263-06	3.9	13.1	4.8	3.1	9.2	1.7	4.0	39.8
711301-05	3.6	14.4	8.8	6.1	19.7	1.7	8.5	62.8
711456-01	7.7	11.4	10.3	7.6	18.3	1.7	9.6	66.6
711319-01	8.6	17.3	10.9	8.1	17.1	1.7	8.3	72.0
711306-08	2.6	10.2	5.8	4.1	6.6	1.7	3.5	34.5
910702-04	2.4	16.4	5.5	3.9	4.3	1.7	3.5	37.7

Figure 6-3 Mixed-Model Commonality

the upper daily rate anticipated for each of the parts or products to be created in the cell. This total demand becomes the designed daily rate (capacity) for the cell, and it is divided into the effective work hours that the cell is planned to be utilized. This will yield a cellular Takt time for all products to be manufactured within the cell, not an individual cycle time of any particular product to be manufactured within the cell. This cellular Takt time is critical in sizing in-process Kanbans based upon any imbalances between the actual times and operational cycle time targets of the cell. This analysis has identified those products that are excellent candidates for a mixed-model cell. It is also essential in identifying the number of machines and people required to support the volume of products to be manufactured within the cell.

Equipment Utilization

Targeted or designed operational cycle time must be calculated within a cell to ensure an efficient utilization. In Demand Flow manufacturing, utilization does not drive the process, but it is a management consideration. Actual operational work content time divided by targeted operational cycle time of the cell will result in the operational machine utilization. If one machine in a cell is not fully utilized, one option would be to have that machine feed additional cells to increase its machine utilization. Line layouts would be adjusted to allow the underutilized machine to feed multiple cells. The cell's resources are calculated by dividing the weighted actual times of the products that require that process by the operational cycle time target.

$$\frac{Actual\ Time\ Weighted}{Operational\ Cycle\ Time} = Resources\ Required$$

Attacking Nonvalue-Added Setups

Both setup steps and maintenance tasks are major factors in machine cells. The reduction or elimination of setup and move time is a primary objective. The process aimed at that end involves:

- Defining the elements of setup

- Sequencing equipment

- Methods analysis

- Advance preparation

- Machine support checklists

During the analysis associated with the TQC sequence of events, the time associated with each setup step is identified. Once this setup has been identified and prioritized, it is methodically attacked. The first step in reducing the setup time is to observe the physical setup being performed. The work to complete the entire setup must be understood by the team responsible for the setup reduction task. After the setup has been physically observed, it is videotaped for a detailed analysis. This detailed analysis will result in the sequence of events required to set up and operate the selected machine.

Each step to set up the machine is classified as either an internal or external step. Internal setup steps are those steps that are performed at the machine and with the machine stopped. External setup steps are those steps that are performed externally to the machine—they can be performed while the machine is producing another part. Internal machine setup steps reduce the time a machine is available to produce parts. Internal setup steps become the highest priority for reduction or elimination. If a setup step cannot be eliminated, it should be moved from internal to external time (reference Figure 6-4).

Tooling required for a machine to produce a part should be pulled to the machine using Kanban techniques. Traditional scheduling systems are nonresponsive and unnecessary. The tool number required to produce a particular part is listed on the Kanban card or container. Once the part is pulled, the Kanban is returned to the producing cell. The machine operator will verify whether or not the tool, identified on the Kanban, is currently at the cell. If the tool is not at the machine cell, the Kanban is directed to the tool and die area to be pulled and returned to the machine cell along with the previously referenced Kanban card.

Checklists

Every machine should have four checklists that are required for the operation and maintenance of the particular machine.

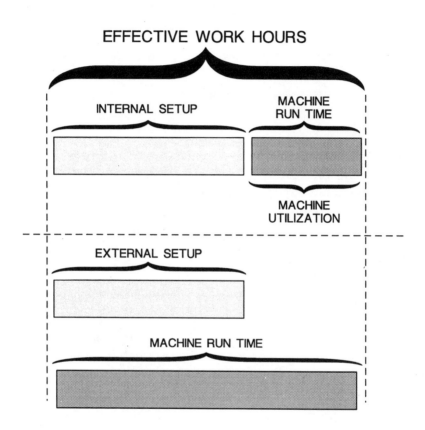

Figure 6-4 Setup Classification

Specifically, every machine should have the following four checklists, or one checklist with four sections:

1. Setup

2. Operation

3. Troubleshooting, in the event of problems

4. Maintenance

Each checklist is specific and requires the operator to verify by checking off each required task performed. This ensures that the process is defined and verifies that the operator has completed required steps before proceeding with the machine operation. Operational method sheets are also utilized to display a graphic image of what the parts will look like, the quality criteria of the part, and what tools should be used. Every effort is made to eliminate guesswork and develop a consistent, predictable and repeatable total quality process.

The first checklist is a list of tasks that the operator will go through to **set up** the particular machine. It will be very specific in sequence and in the tasks to be performed, and it will have a physical check box for key items that operators are required to perform during the setup tasks. The second checklist is an **operational** list of tasks that must be followed during the start-up and operation of a particular machine. This checklist will identify the specific sequence an operator must go through before the machine is allowed to produce the first part in the shift. The third checklist required to support a machine is a **troubleshooting** checklist. This checklist is used in the event there is a problem during the setup or the routine operation of the machine. This checklist will guide operators through a process of identifying the possible cause of a particular problem and assist in setting priorities for the things that need to be verified before proceeding with the checklist.

Bibles of Machine Operation

If the troubleshooting checklist identifies a problem and it is solved by the operator, then the operator can continue with the operational checklist and bring up the machine. The fourth checklist required to support the machine is the **maintenance** checklist. This will identify the likely causes of problems that stop the operator during the setup or operational aspects of the machine. The maintenance checklist is designed to be used by the maintenance person who performs the predictive and preventative maintenance program, and it will identify the likely cause of the problem that is being analyzed at that time on the machine. Special tools and parts required to support the machine should be kept near the machine, readily available to the maintenance mechanic. The objective is to be able to fix the machine and bring it back on line as quickly as possible.

Machine Maintenance

Total preventative maintenance is a very important part of Demand Flow manufacturing. It is extremely important that the machines used in the process are maintained so that they will remain available for use during production. Machines should be standardized according to type and manufacturer. Machines that eliminate internal setup and are very reliable and easy to maintain are preferred over large, powerful machines that can be set up to do multiple functional machining tasks.

Routine maintenance, such as checking pressure settings, temperatures and chain or sprocket tensions, should be performed by the employees who operate the machines before the equipment is started for the production shift. The machine operator will go through a routine checklist that identifies the specific sequence and tasks that must be verified before the machine can be operated. Once the operator has completed the routine maintenance and filled out the operational checklist, the machine can be operated.

An Integral Demand Flow Manufacturing Requirement

Total preventive maintenance is an essential part of flow manufacturing. The program includes:

- A pre-operational checklist for machine operators;

- Immediate verification of emergency failures against the checklist—preventative and predictive maintenance programs;

- Emergency maintenance analysis;

- Undercapacity scheduling;

- Corresponding scheduled maintenance programs, which are all viewed as key to improved product quality and reduced in-process inventory.

The objective with predictive and preventative maintenance programs is to increase the machine up-time, eliminate the need for emergency maintenance, and make the machine more predictable over a period of time. As the predictive and preventative maintenance programs improve, machine utilization will improve, and in-process inventories can be reduced. Adjustments must be made for machines that routinely go down for maintenance problems. As an example, if it routinely takes 20 minutes per shift to repair a machine and bring it back on line, effective work hours per shift for that particular machine should be adjusted downward by the 15 or 20 minutes that the machine is anticipated to be down. This could result in a shorter designed operational cycle time for this particular machine as opposed to the rest of the cell or flow process that it supports. This would also require a corresponding in-process Kanban between the machine and its supporting processes to buffer the nonproductive period of time that the machine is unavailable.

Demand Flow Line and Cell Designs

Demand Flow manufacturing is the technological bonding of a flexible production flow process to a demand pull material system. The DFT production flow process is based upon in-process total quality control at the point where the work is performed. The flow line or cell layouts are a result of the techniques of cycle time line designs. These flow manufacturing techniques include:

- TQC sequence of events

- Daily rates

- Operational and total product cycle time

- TQC operations

- Kanban

- Flexible people and machines

- Linear flow line layouts

Flexible pull lines and cells with a focus on the elimination of nonvalue-added steps are keys to many of the flow manufacturing benefits: to drastically reduce work-in-process dollars, reduce floor space, reduce scrap/rework, reduce finished goods inventory dollars, reduce overhead, and reduce computer activity and transactions. Product costs are reduced while the product quality is improved, thereby enhancing a corporation's ability to compete. *Manufacturing can now become a corporation's strategic weapon!*

Chapter Seven

Product Design for Demand Flow Manufacturing

Speed-to-Market will be the key strategic weapon for *world-class* manufacturing companies in the 1990s and beyond. Product development time and the time to get products through manufacturing to customers must be significantly reduced. Reductions of five or ten percent will be inadequate. Reductions of 50 percent or more are necessary to remain competitive in the worldwide marketplace. Design engineering can no longer afford to be an isolated and slow moving organization. Product designs must be cost effective, designed for high quality flow production, and manufacturable upon product release. Engineering can no longer function in a design vacuum but must be part of the total company Demand Flow manufacturing technology.

Once a product is introduced, the manner in which documentation is released and the manner in which engineering change is controlled are drastically simplified to become more effective and consistent with the Demand Flow manufacturing technology.

Speed-to-Market

The *world-class* manufacturer must reduce the total time it takes from the start of the research and development cycle to the completion of a released product from manufacturing. Technology turnover is the total life cycle of a product from the time development begins to the end of the product sales cycle. The challenge to the *world-class* manufacturer is to minimize the development and pre-production release portion of the technology turnover cycle and to increase the sales portion. The longer the sales cycle of a product, the greater the profit will be for the company. If a company is first to introduce a product into the marketplace, initial prices can be higher and market share can increase. Eventually, when the competition enters the marketplace, all manufacturers must become competitive producers. If the Demand Flow manufacturer can be first to market and have a quick delivery cycle through manufacturing, the manufacturer can use this as a very powerful, competitive tool. Once the product is released to manufacturing, it must be producible and functional upon design release. While the volume of engineering changes for new products can be expected to remain high, the initial quality of the product and the functionality, as perceived by the customer, must be *world-class*.

Technology turnover cycles are increasing as each life cycle is becoming shorter and shorter. Although the United States may be the technology leader in the world, it falls well behind major competitors in the actual implementation of the technology. Many companies are unable to recoup even research and development expenditures with product sales because of lengthy product introductions.

Design and Manufacturing as a Team

The *world-class* company must break the partitions between product and process design and have a free flow of information, people, methods and tools between design engineering and manufacturing. These two, jointly, must develop both products and processes that are consistently linked to ensure the highest quality at the lowest cost for the shortest possible throughput time between manufacturing and the marketplace. Engineers must take into account a design for total quality and eliminate inspection steps with a design-for-producibility focus. Manufacturing engineering and quality must be involved at an early stage of the design cycle to ensure that a total quality product is indeed producible in manufacturing. They will be deeply involved in the prototype and other cycles in advance of new product release. Again, *speed-to-market* is the key to competitive survival.

Technology Turnover Transfer Teams

Marketing will initially work with the outside customers to develop a product specification. The product specification will identify the customer specification, the market, the competition, the price and product expectations. At this point, top management will select a transfer team leader to cross all functional boundaries to get a quality product to market as quickly as possible. Design engineering will develop a product design based upon the product specifications. At this point in the process, marketing, design engineering, and the transfer team leader are assigned to the "transfer team" (reference Figure 7-1).

The product design will identify product targets in the areas of cost, performance and specifications. At this point, general component availability will be analyzed. Design engineering should, wherever possible, use existing components selected from preferred suppliers. Based upon the product design, quality engineering will then join the transfer team and jointly, along with design engineering, develop a quality specification for the product and for the process.

Quality Expectations Determined

In the next phase the transfer team will analyze the customer expectations and the product specifications and verify that they are consistent. Also at this phase, component specifications will be drafted. Customers should be invited to preview the product specifications and determine whether or not they meet their expectations. Supplier availability will also be re-

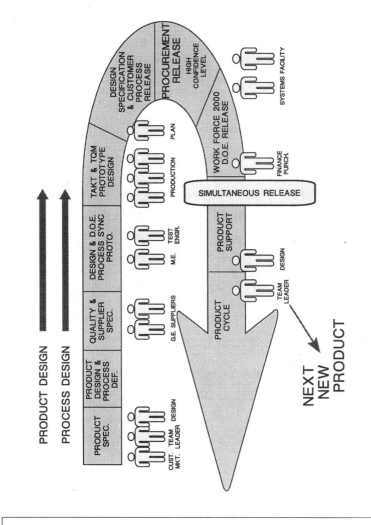

Figure 7-1 Transfer Team Organizations

viewed. If not, the team must revisit the product specification phase of the development process. If the product and design specifications are consistent and approved, a design prototype will be produced to meet the design specifications. Then a manufacturing engineer and a test engineer will join the transfer team. At this phase, the transfer team will begin to work on the TQC sequence of events, identifying process specifications and looking for designed-for-defect problems that should be eliminated in the design prototype phase. TQC sequence of events will be completed at this phase. If a total quality process flow cannot be defined, manufacturing cannot produce the product and a return to the product design or product specification phase of the development process must be made. The product produced during the design prototype phase will ensure that the product meets customer and design specifications.

Developing the Initial Demand Flow Process

If the design prototype passes this test, the next phase will produce a manufacturing prototype. This can be built in a laboratory or model shop environment utilizing special equipment and extra-talented production personnel. This prototype will prove the component specifications, manufacturing documentation, process capability and equipment tooling. If it can't be produced with material bought to the component specifications, using the TQC sequence of events, using manufacturing equipment and tooling, along with gifted production personnel, the process would return to the product design phase. At this phase, the TQC operational method sheets will start to be created. During the manufacturing prototype phase, the capacity of the process required to support customer demands will be determined. Operational cycle time will be calculated and targeted. A flat, "pile of parts," bill of material will be created and approved. At this point, method sheets will be reviewed and a determination will be made to ensure that there is a producible TQC design. If the producibility test is successfully met, component specification documentation can be released. Also during this phase, a planning/materials person is added to the transfer team.

Design for Total Quality

The *world-class* flow process is one of *total quality*. Whenever there is more than one way to perform a task, but only one of the ways is correct, a subsequent validation step will be required. Assembly tasks should not be designed to allow the production employees to make a wrong decision. Symmetrical designs that enable an employee to assemble a part incorrectly will require a later TQC approval in the flow process. If a person had multiple ways to perform work, but only one way was correct, and the person completed the work and covered up the work, the product created in this process would be classified as "designed for defect." In this example, the operation that completed the work cannot perform the TQC approval of the work. If there is only one way to assemble a part, a symmetrical design, then a single operation can perform and verify the work. Products must be designed utilizing techniques that will allow the total quality and verification steps to function correctly. Of course, a design that permits work to be performed in only one way—the right way—is preferred.

Parts Standardization is Essential

It also should be a goal of design engineering to standardize material into as few part numbers as possible. If the manufacturer is already using five different lengths of similar plastic tubing on existing products, these similar parts must be reviewed for standardization before a sixth length of tubing is designed into a new product. Design engineering should be aware of which parts are being used in manufacturing and which preferred suppliers are on DFT contracts. They will not sacrifice product quality when they standardize to preferred suppliers by eliminating components and increasing component volumes with preferred suppliers. Standardization produces a higher volume per part, and typically the higher the volume of a part, the lower the price.

Focus on Suppliers

Supplier management is greatly enhanced with a smaller part number base. As purchasing drives the total number of suppliers down and begins to focus on total cost, design engineering should focus on using these preferred suppliers in new product designs wherever possible.

Components with long lead time requirements will be purchased, component specifications will be finalized, suppliers will be approved, transportation networks will be set up, packaging specifications to facilitate dock to RIP deliveries will be defined, and flexible DFT contracts will be established for major suppliers. There should be, at this stage, a high confidence level in the product and process design. If there is not, a return to the manufacturing prototype phase is required.

Preparing for Release

During the pre-production phase prior to production release, all of the elements come together. Method sheets are approved and released based upon the targeted operational cycle time. Demand Flow lines have been designed based upon the shortest total product cycle time. Kanbans, both raw materials and in-process, are sized and placed; flexible employees are being cross-trained one-up, one-down in the process. Any final product or process bugs are worked out at this stage. Finance, systems and facilities people are brought onto the transfer team to review the pre-production release from their functional perspectives. At this time, the standard product cost is established replacing the transfer team's previous estimates. Checklists to support the production machines are completed and released.

At the pre-production phase a small quantity of products will be manufactured and released to customers. These products will be built using the regular production employees, the planned production machines, released tooling, components purchased to released specification drawings, and TQC operational method sheets. They will be produced out of the "real" production flow process. Process capabilities will also be validated during this phase. These units built during the pre-production stage must meet the design specifications using components and materials purchased to the component/materials specifications. If the product meets the design specifications, minor changes can be made at this stage prior to the actual design release.

Product Release and Acceptance

The product is now ready for design release. The customer will be involved in the final acceptance phase of the product. Engineering change activity will be high for the initial release phase, so the transfer team design members will remain on the team for the initial three to six months following the product release. The manufacturing flow process is now fine-tuned between operations. Employee involvement will begin to improve the process and begin to reduce in-process and material Kanbans closer to the calculated levels as the product and the process quickly mature. The product is designed and released for the manufacturing flow process. This ensures a *total quality* and producible product upon design release. The "transfer team" technology can improve a company's *speed-to-market,* thereby becoming a very powerful and competitive weapon for the *world-class* company.

Organizational Impacts

The functional boundaries and systems inherent to the traditional product development process are a major cause for the lengthy product introduction cycles and eventual marketplace failures. Organizationally in Demand Flow manufacturing, transfer team members report to the team leader while the product is being developed. This is not a dotted line reporting relationship, but a hard line. The transfer team leader must have the responsibility and authority to get a quality product to market as quickly as possible. The transfer team leader will be reporting to design engineering until product release. Then the team leader, along with all team members, will report to the manufacturing vice president or director after the product is released. The design engineer and team leader will work, under the team leader, in manufacturing for the initial period after product release; then eventually they will rotate back into design engineering onto another transfer team for the next product introduction. The primary reporting and responsibility of transfer team members must be to the product and the transfer team, not to a functional organization.

Demand Flow Manufacturing Product Fundamentals

The bill of material for Demand Flow manufacturing tends to be very flat—there are no subassemblies. This is in marked contrast to traditional functional schedulized manufacturing which has subassemblies and fabricated parts structured into higher level subassemblies and fabricated parts, several times over. In traditional schedulized manufacturing, the bill of material drives the process; in Demand Flow manufacturing, the operational cycle time drives the work content and the bill of material becomes a basic "pile of parts." The bill of material in a Demand Flow environment is quite different from the functional bill of material now used in traditional manufacturing. The bill of material in a flow process is the fundamental building block of the product—it is the recipe of purchased materials to be consumed by the process in order to manufacture a product. There are several differences between the Demand Flow manufacturing bill of material and the traditional multilevel bill of material.

Subassembly Versus Flat

The Demand Flow manufacturing bill of material will approach a single-level, flat pile of parts that contains only the purchased components that are required to build the product. Unlike traditional functional manufacturing, there are neither subassemblies nor phantoms in Demand Flow manufacturing. It is the multilevel subassembly of traditional manufacturing versus the flat pile of parts of Demand Flow manufacturing. In traditional manufacturing, the product design is functional with parts grouped into subassemblies or fabricated machine parts (reference Figure 7-2).

These subassemblies and fabricated parts are scheduled, issued, tracked and costed as separate entities. The top-level model number will be the same whether or not there are

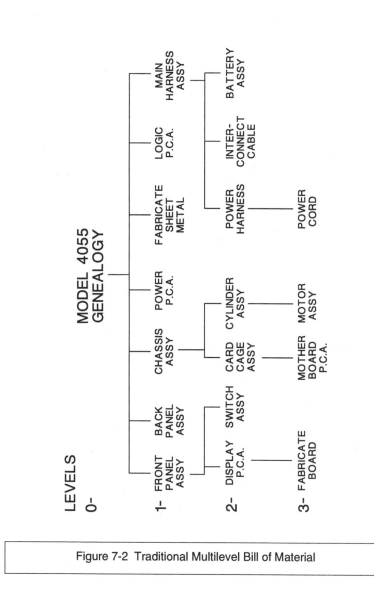

Figure 7-2 Traditional Multilevel Bill of Material

subassemblies structured below it. Subassembly part numbers are internal tracking and collection identities that do not add value to the product. Often, the subassemblies are departmentalized with some being built in one department and others being built in another. In such cases, the subassemblies are sent to Work-In-Process (WIP) storerooms and later issued to the consuming departments.

Because of the departmentalization, the process layout is basically driven by the bill of material—the design, manufacturing process and layout are all functional. In Demand Flow manufacturing, the bill of material is a listing of the purchased parts required to build a product. Where they are assembled in the process is not relevant to the bill of material. Component parts or materials can be moved around, for the purposes of line balancing, without affecting the bill of material. Process improvements can be made without complicated engineering change orders. This becomes an uncoupling of the process and the functional bill of material.

Disconnected Parts

In Demand Flow manufacturing, the bill of material is a disconnected pile of parts; in traditional manufacturing, the bill of material drives the schedulized production process. In Demand Flow manufacturing, there is no need for the subassembly bill of material. Operational cycle time dictates the work content per operation and all operations are documented on TQC operational method sheets. There is no scheduling, no picking of subassembly kits of parts, and no functional production departments. Beyond the functional design prototype phase, there is no need for the multilevel bill of material. Of course, there is no need for a corresponding subassembly drawing, *ever!* In discussions about the "levels" of a traditional bill of material, the top, or model, level of the product bill of material is referred to as level "0." The purchased parts, subassemblies and fabricated parts that are directly structured to the model number are considered to be in level "1." Typically, additional lower level purchased parts, subassemblies or fabricated parts are structured to high-level subassemblies creating a multilevel product bill of material.

Functional Design Versus Demand Flow Technology and Simultaneous Engineering

For years we have designed and manufactured products using the functional multilevel bill of material. These subassembly or machining-level part numbers are necessary to schedule, pick kits of parts, issue material, and to route in-process production in traditional manufacturing. Design engineering releases these functional multilevel bills of material and maintains a documentation control system for each of these multilevel assemblies and fabricated parts. Computerized scheduling systems (MRP II) have been developed to assist in the planning, scheduling and control of these multilevel bills of material. Traditional costing and management systems have been developed based upon this multilevel bill of material philosophy. Complicated and expensive engineering change systems have been developed to attempt to control these complex multilevel bills of material.

In Demand Flow manufacturing, operational cycle time will define the targeted work content. Material will be pulled to the operation where the work is performed using Kanban techniques. Since the Demand Flow manufacturer does not schedule, pick kits of parts or build subassemblies, there is no manufacturing need for a multilevel bill of material. Since the transfer team designed and developed a product for Demand Flow manufacturing, design engineering does not require a multilevel bill of material either. There can only be one consistent philosophy for the design, development, release and manufacturing of products within the *world-class* company.

Product Bill of Material

All products that are forecast by marketing or customer service and sold to customers will have a bill of material. This includes:

- Top-level products — model numbers

- Options to standard products

- Field replaceable units — FRUs, or spares

Final products will have a model number that is used by marketing to sell the product to a customer. This model number is printed in the sales and marketing literature, and it usually *does not change* during the life of the product. This model number is the communication identity among the manufacturer and the customer, distributors, order entry, and top management reporting. This final product model number has a top-level part number that is used to control the design and manufacturing of the product (reference Figure 7-3).

Field Replaceable Units

A Field Replaceable Unit (FRU) is an interchangeable portion of a top-level product for field service or customer service usage. FRUs are products that are sold and forecasted by marketing separately from the complete final product. They are not subassemblies of traditional manufacturing. They have a separate and distinct bill of material which may or may not share common parts with the final or original end product. FRUs are *not* tied to the top-level product bill of material. FRUs, or spares, may be required at a later date based upon the service nature of the original product. It is a totally independent portion of a final product. It can be built in the same or in a totally independent process from the final product. It is something that marketing will sell and customers will buy separately. The product and FRU may have common parts, but the FRU is not structured as a subassembly to the final product (reference Figure 7-4).

An example of a FRU is the engine of a lawn mower. The engine and lawn mower are originally sold together, and a similar engine is later sold separately for replacement by field service. It would not be unusual for both the product and the

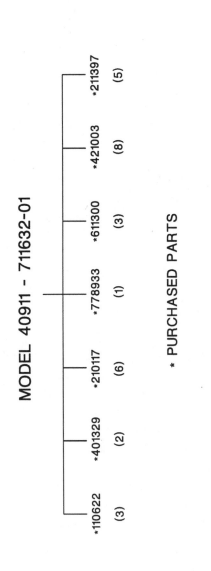

Figure 7-3 Top-level Product Bill of Material

FRU to have some common parts, such as pistons, nuts, and bolts. The FRU will always have additional costs, parts, and instruction manuals to control the replacement process by the field service people. Additional testing and production time, shipping materials, and identification labels may be associated with the FRU and not with the final product.

Customers may order spare printed circuit boards to quickly repair a system that was installed at an earlier date. The field service organization may also want spare components of a product so that if a component fails, the field service person can conduct repairs at the customer's site without sending the entire unit back to the factory for repair. Some industries or products have FRUs, others do not. Aircraft, computers, and automobiles are examples of products that have FRUs; a spark plug and wooden pencil are examples of products that do not have FRUs. FRUs can be built on the same line or independently, whichever is preferred, and FRUs can either be manufactured or purchased parts. The independence between the FRU and the product, from a bill of material standpoint, is further illustrated by the fact that a change can be made at one date on a FRU and at an entirely different date, or not at all, on the final product. Additionally, the FRU is likely to contain some bill of material information that is different from the information on the product bill of material. That includes a packing container, label, installation instructions, and documentation required by the FRU, which may not be a part of the original product bill of material.

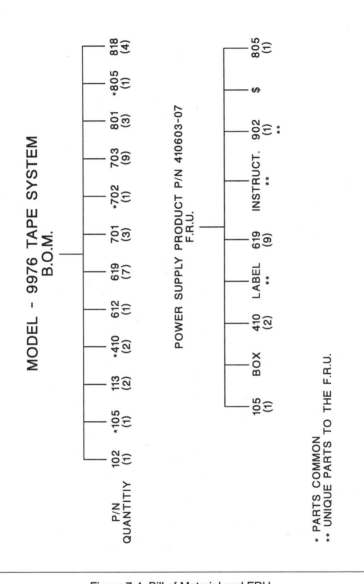

Figure 7-4 Bill of Material and FRU

Compression of the Multilevel Bill of Material

Traditional companies have "always" designed products using multilevel bills of material that are scheduled, issued, tracked and costed accordingly. When implementing Demand Flow Technology the bill of material is flattened or compressed to a single-level pile of purchased parts. If the product has a FRU, a separate bill of material will be created for it. Whether or not a product has an associated FRU, all of the purchased components will be structured at the bill of material of the top-level product. Compressing the bill of material can be easily accomplished with one engineering change that obsoletes the subassembly drawings and brings all purchased parts to the top-level product. Any drawing IDs to a former subassembly can be saved for historical tracking purposes. The compression of the multilevel bill of material should not be a major implementation stumbling block. The product has not changed identity at all, only how it is documented internally within the manufacturing company.

Flattening out the bill of material is a major change in thinking for the traditional manufacturer who has always done it otherwise. Progressive engineering and manufacturing personnel who have attempted to maintain the traditional multilevel bill of material will push to implement the "flat" Demand Flow manufacturing bill of material for their own benefit as well as that of the company. On the other hand, traditional political employees and managers who resist change or are unwilling to or incapable of accepting change will provide numerous and continuous roadblocks to breaking "the

way we've always done it." This topic can become an opportunity for a personal or political win with a resulting loss to the
company.

Phantom Bills of Material

Some traditional manufacturers are very cautious about
implementing Demand Flow manufacturing and about flattening the bill of material. These manufacturers attempt to evolve
into Demand Flow manufacturing just by reducing lot sizes,
e.g., "MRP II, Lot Size of 1." Typically, they will attempt to go
to a "blow throughout, make on, or phantom" bill of material.
These phantom subassemblies still appear on the higher level
subassembly's bill of material; however, the scheduling system
(MRP II) ignores them and does not try to open up work orders
to issue material for the phantom assemblies. This is an unac-
ceptable and dangerous approach, since all of the complex
problems associated with engineering changes, effectivity dates
and documentation systems related to a multilevel bill of material will remain. In addition, flow line design, method sheet
management, cycle time calculations, work balancing and
backflush control are unnecessarily complicated by these subassemblies, whether or not they are called a phantom. This
misinformed approach to flattening the bill of material should
be avoided.

Since the "flat" bill of material is a key in the transition
from traditional to *world-class* Demand Flow Technology, it
will immediately affect several traditional departments and

organizations. Failure to solve this key element of the implementation may be an indication of a lack of support, understanding and commitment from top management.

Multipurpose Bill of Material

The bill of material in Demand Flow manufacturing serves dual purposes: it not only identifies the parts required to build a product, but it is also used to relieve the inventory of the parts/materials consumed when the product is completed. This flow manufacturing technique is referred to as backflush inventory control. This inventory control information is referenced on the bill of material as a backflush location. Inventory control systems directly utilize the DFT bill of material to relieve the on-hand quantity of inventory from RIP. Thus, it is mandatory to have a correct bill of material in order to ensure accurate on-hand inventories in RIP. Traditionally, attempts to compensate for an incorrect bill of material include additional transactions, such as miscellaneous issues or unplanned issues from a storeroom. In Demand Flow manufacturing the assumption is made that if the product was built, the parts on the bill of material were consumed. If the bill of material is incorrect, inventory will be consumed incorrectly and the wrong information will be fed to the procurement system for component replenishment. From a company purchasing standpoint, the bill of material is used to determine which parts to buy and when they must be delivered.

Managing Engineering Change in
Demand Flow Manufacturing

Another major difference between the Demand Flow manufacturing and traditional bills of material is that with Demand Flow manufacturing, the engineering change system can utilize the "pending change" implementation techniques. This enables the Demand Flow manufacturer to approve an engineering change prior to assigning an effectivity date or a corresponding revision level of incorporation. The new materials can be ordered, but the higher level revision level is not assigned until the change is ready to be implemented. Properly implementing an engineering change with a traditional multi-level subassembly bill of material can be a coordination nightmare. Effectively, each level of the multilevel bill of material must be coordinated with each lower level. Part number changes to a lower level component can cascade up to higher levels. Multiple changes to a multilevel product, attempted at different times with different effective dates, can border on the impossible from a configuration control standpoint. So, the traditional manufacturers typically will attempt to use product deviations to try to stem the cascading effects of these changes. An outdated company may still attempt to use the "birthing" technique in which changes are queued for a product and implemented all at once. Most products must improve and change rapidly, and the volume of engineering changes can remain high for some products. With the single-level bill of material, engineering changes become simple and effective.

Any change that affects the form, fit or function of a product must have an accompanying Engineering Change Order (ECO) that is approved by design engineering. Process changes which do not in any way affect product form, fit or function may follow a more streamlined system. However, caution should be exercised in order to be certain that form, fit or function is not violated. Design engineering review may be appropriate, but this must be done in an expeditious manner. Process changes will be implemented, throughout the day, in a day or less.

Backflush Effectivity

When engineering indicates a new part will be introduced into a product via an ECO, the change is assigned an engineering change number and approved through normal approval channels. Upon ECO approval, the new part that needs to be procured will be input as a "pending change" to the planning system with an *estimated* delivery date. The buyer will then go out and procure the new part called out on the engineering change. However, this pending change does not affect the revision level of the product, nor is the current bill of material information changed. The engineering change order is "pending" until the required material is received and the change is actually implemented. If a different engineering change is approved prior to receipt of the new part associated with the first change and this second engineering change part is immediately available, then the second engineering change would be assigned the next revision level when it is implemented. The first engineering change is still considered pending until its part arrives. In schedulized manufacturing (MRP II), having an effective date to the week or work order is typically sufficient. In Demand Flow manufacturing, when the manufacturer is ready to implement the change, the first unit going through the process with the change will be tagged with the engineering change number that authorized the change.

When this tagged unit reaches the point of backflush, only then does the higher level revision get incorporated. The revision level is assigned, the bill of material is updated, the pending change is removed, and the material associated with the bill of material is correctly backflushed. This technique is known as "backflush effectivity." It requires the changed unit to be produced in a flow process sequentially which, in Demand Flow manufacturing, is the way the units are manufactured. If another change is to be made, the same process is followed. Revision levels are assigned sequentially as the change is actually implemented.

Changing Form, Fit or Function

The Demand Flow manufacturing flat bill of material facilitates immediate and future engineering changes in a way that is easier, faster and more accurate than that imaginable by the more complex multilevel bill of material. This is because of its flat nature and because it does not contain the traditional interrelationships of the multilevels and the corresponding domino effect of change. If an engineering change is made that affects the form, fit or function of a product, the component and higher level product part numbers must be changed. If an engineering change is made that does not impact the form, fit or function, that change is simply a revision change to the part number, and its higher level product will not be affected. Part number revisions are never shown on a Kanban. Revision changes are always documented on an ECO, and they should never have a rework disposition for on-hand or in-process material.

Planning Bill of Material

If a product has several hundred different options, the possible number of unique products to document, plan, build and cost could become unwieldy. In these cases where there are highly optioned products, a planning bill of material is used to identify the common part for each product. Individual bills of material for the options would be backflushed separately. The product could be configured at order entry to include the base product and the specific options for this sales order. The sales order which is configured would take on a unique number identity. The sales order (sales order number) would be back-flushed at completion. This basic product bill of material would be a "pile of parts" with an independent bill of material for each option.

Plethora of Options

An example is the auto industry in which there may be dozens of different colors; dozens of different tape, radio and sound systems; dozens of different kinds and colors of interiors; dozens of different kinds of wheels and tires; and so forth. A flat bill of material for each possible combination would prove unwieldy and unnecessarily complicated. This can be dangerous, and caution should be used. On the other hand, products with possible options numbering 20 or 25 are not sufficient to force a planning bill of material. Dictating a planning bill of material is a step that should only be required with a large number of options or combinations of options.

Independent Processes and Divisions

If a company produces a product in a flow process, with feeder lines attached and pulled into the final product, its product bill of material should be a pile of purchased parts. If a company has a centralized product design engineering, along with multiple independent divisions, this will create a multi-level bill of material. This is the case in divisions which are managed independently and controlled by a central product design group. The divisions have independent finance, planning and management and, indeed, can make a profit on products sent to other divisions. In these cases, design engineering should structure a part number for the assembly produced in one division and sold to another internal plant (reference Figure 7-5).

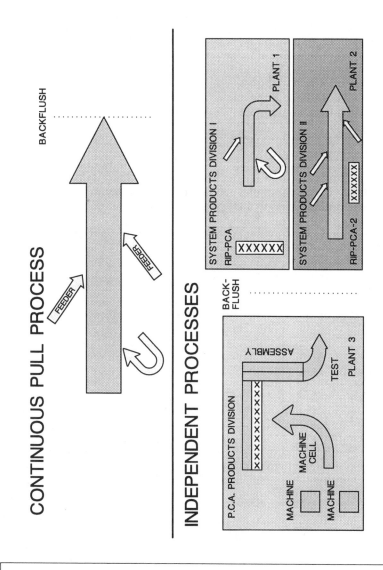

Figure 7-5 Independent Divisions and Products

As an example, let's use an independent feeder division that is manufacturing printed circuit boards and sending them to an independent systems plant that is an internal division of the corporation. Since there is one central product design, a corporate two-level bill of material will result. To the printed circuit board division, their bill of material is a pile of components to make the assembly. To the system division, one of the purchased parts they procure is a printed circuit board assembly, which just so happens to come from a supplier division. The system division has a flat bill of material as well. To the corporation, a two-level bill of material has been designed.

Demand Flow Manufacturing Documentation

Documentation utilized by the Demand Flow manufacturer will change from the traditional documentation systems used today. As the bill of material is compressed, subassembly drawings are no longer required. Visual, graphic method sheets replace traditional assembly instructions that are loaded with text which most employees avoid reading. Engineering changes which affect form, fit or function of a product will continue to be controlled by design engineering. A method ID is related to the components on the bill of material. This will enable engineering to do a "part number/where used" on method IDs. When the engineering change is approved, the process documents that need to be modified will already be identified. Process changes which do not affect form, fit or function of a product will be controlled by manufacturing engineering and will tend to be frequent and quick to implement. Method sheets will tell the operator what to do and what to inspect or validate.

Causes for defects on current products will be identified via the methodization and employee involvement processes. While design engineering must continue to develop new products, it must also place renewed priority on existing products to correct design problems. While not all changes can be made immediately, design engineering must become an integral part of the continuous improvement process. The "throwing products over the fence to manufacturing, then proceeding with the next new product" mentality should be avoided.

Methodizing the Process

The Demand Flow manufacturer will "methodize" the process one time based upon the highest desired rate and shortest cycle time possible. The calculated work content is an operation, and the documentation of the work is an operational method sheet. If an engineering change order is approved, a method sheet may have to be changed, but only those method sheets that are affected by the change order would be changed. The Demand Flow process is designed and "methodized" one time; however, changes to operational method sheets will be done frequently based upon the engineering change orders and the employee improvement programs. Verification and TQC points must also be clearly colored on the method sheet. The Demand Flow manufacturer is imbedding quality into the process rather than relying on external inspection. The TQC operational method sheets will guide the operator to these points. Employees may verify their own work; however, TQC points are validations of work performed at a prior operation. If a TQC point is covered up and cannot be verified, this is identified as an Acceptable Quality Level (AQL) product containing a design for defect that will be assigned to design engineering.

TQC Operational Method Sheets

TQC operational method sheets are used to communicate graphically to the production employees precisely what they are to do in terms of work content, verification and total quality control (reference Figures 7-6 and 7-7).

Each is created directly from the TQC sequence of events. The sheets should have minimal text on them. The sheets are dominated by illustrations of the unit showing the work to be done at that station, how it is to be done, and what is to be verified against work performed at this operation. Work content is coded yellow, work to verify is coded blue, and work on which total quality control is performed is coded red. The find number, part number, description and quantity of each part is listed, as is the process point, product and operation number. There is no guesswork, and there are no red lines, alterations or modifications on the method sheets. If changes are to be made, the sheets are to be redone. The operator is not left with a sheet full of pencil scratches wondering which change was the latest and who authorized it.

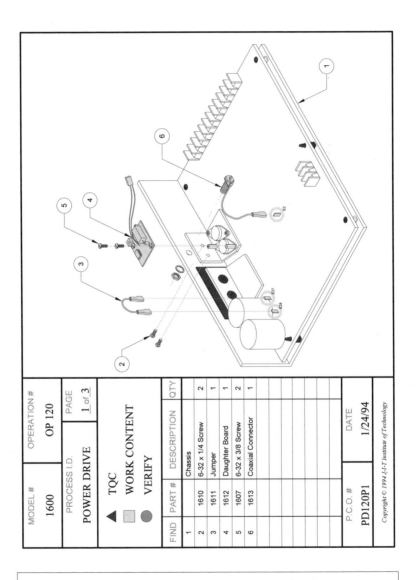

Figure 7-6 TQC Operational Method Sheet

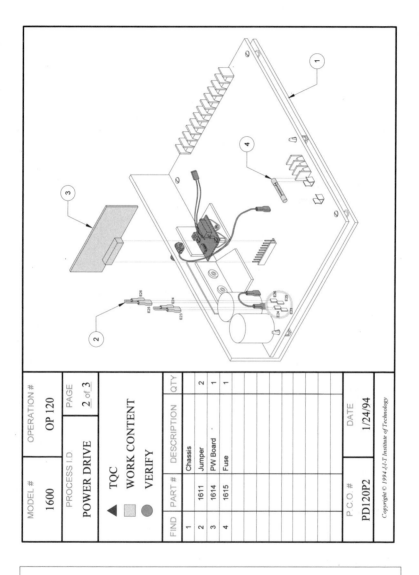

Figure 7-7 TQC Operational Method Sheet

Demand Flow Manufacturing Systems Integration

Formal computer tools are available to the *world-class* manufacturer to create an effective documentation network. The Computer-Aided Design (CAD) system can be interfaced with the pile of parts bill of material and operational method sheet IDs to download component drawings and specifications, as well as quality specifications. This will enable the manufacturing and quality engineer to utilize the design specification documentation as an aid to create bills of material and method sheets quickly. However, the creation and maintenance of operational method sheets should not be attempted in CAD. Far more cost effective PC-based graphic applications are readily available.

PC-based LAN "methods network" can also be created. This network should be interfaced to the bill of material so that when an engineering change is generated, the appropriate method sheet changes can be automatically found and updated. The method network will link graphic software to hardcopy output devices with an objective of being able to make a method sheet change and getting it to the production floor in 30 minutes or less. Interfacing to the manufacturing system mainframe is another possible application. PC networking technology can be incorporated quickly without large investments in hardware or software.

Only One Bill of Material

There is only one bill of material in a *world-class* manufacturing environment—there is not a design bill of material and a manufacturing bill of material. The problem with the multiple bill of material is that it is not possible to keep the information totally consistent. While the pile of parts information and specifications are clearly under design engineering control, other elements associated with the bill of material, such as backflush and method information, are maintained by manufacturing. There should be only one bill of material that is shared by all. The bill of material is 100 percent accurate, and it can never become inconsistent, since there is only one companywide bill of material.

Chapter Eight

World-Class Procurement Forecasting and Quality Source Management

U nfortunately, some manufacturing companies choose suppliers and the procurement process as the place to begin their Demand Flow Technology implementation program. These companies are under the misconception that Demand Flow Technology creates an inventory reduction program that forces the suppliers to carry inventory instead of the consuming manufacturer. The program sounds attractive on the surface: drive down your inventory investment via more frequent deliveries, reduce costs via negotiated agreements based on higher volume, and receive higher quality material based upon tightening specifications and elimination of inspection. This is a highly attractive, alluring prospect. It is also a very dangerous trap.

Suppliers Are Not Warehouses

Demand Flow manufacturing should never start with suppliers, and effective procurement programs should never drive suppliers beyond the capabilities of the consuming manufacturer's own internal process. It is of little benefit to insist on daily deliveries from suppliers while your own manufacturing process is still scheduling, picking kits and building multilevel subassemblies. Transportation costs can rise as deliveries increase, and without a freight program that is geared to reducing total transportation costs, this can increase overall product costs. Reducing lot sizes and increasing deliveries can increase storeroom transactions and costs. Elimination of incoming and/or in-process inspectors without first ensuring a quality part and process at the supplier will result in finding any defective purchased materials in the product assembly process. Adverse scrap and rework costs will occur.

Closer Relationship

Demand Flow manufacturing procurement programs can be effective only as part of an integrated company implementation viewing material suppliers as an extension of the Demand Flow production process. The basic premise of the buyer/supplier relationship must shift from a somewhat antagonistic, price-based stance to a cooperative relationship based on mutual benefit. Personnel in the procurement department will find their roles changing as well. Buyers will spend far less time order launching and expediting and more time on flexibility management, contract negotiation, and packaging and transportation aspects of the procurement process.

Leery Suppliers Need Education

As the internal Demand Flow Technology implementation begins with defining the sequence of events, defining cycle times and points of Kanban, and methodizing, so, too, will begin the process of educating suppliers. Suppliers must gain a basic understanding of flow strategies and technology. Suppliers must also be told that, although the company is not operating under Demand Flow manufacturing today, it is moving swiftly and directly toward becoming a Demand Flow manufacturer. One of the most misunderstood and misused aspects of DFT is supplier management. Many suppliers are extremely cautious about flow (J-I-T) manufacturing because they have the erroneous impression that it is a program requiring them to store buyers' inventory. Suppliers see that they are asked to make frequent deliveries, sometimes daily, and to produce 100 percent defect-free materials while reducing costs. Demand Flow manufacturing expands the in-process quality and material pull techniques back to the source for higher quality and lower cost materials. The supplier becomes an extension of the manufacturing process in a relationship that tends to be more mutually advantageous. Many of the guidelines for the relationship between the Demand Flow manufacturer and supplier are predicated on common goals, mutual trust and mutual advantage.

Use Supplier Expertise

Every effort should be made to design parts that are easily produced. Standardized components should be selected, making sure that there are no variances between the supplier specifications and manufacturer requirements. Design engineering should try to use existing preferred components wherever possible. Suppliers should be urged to participate in part selection and design. In many respects, no one knows better how to select components and meet specifications or is better positioned for recommending modifications than the supplier. The *world-class* manufacturer seeks a consistent approach to standardization and meeting specification of material to be used in all phases of the design cycle and the procurement process.

Supplier Cooperation

The concept of the relationship with suppliers in Demand Flow manufacturing is not one of pressuring the supplier or trying to increase supplier costs by having them hold the manufacturer's inventory. The objective is not to force the supplier to build a plant near the manufacturer's operation or otherwise have the supplier store its inventory. The new relationship with the supplier starts very slowly. The Demand Flow manufacturer must start with its own internal process. Ninety-percent-plus internal linearity must be achieved before the suppliers are pulled directly into the process.

A "Supplier Day" is held at the Demand Flow manufacturer's plant. The suppliers are told all about the Demand Flow process and strategies. Data are exchanged; implementation plans and schedules are shared. The suppliers will not be forced to convert to Demand Flow manufacturing, but they understand that it is preferred.

Promote Understanding

It is important that the suppliers understand the Demand Flow manufacturing philosophy and associated technology used in the Demand Flow manufacturer's plant and processes. This will assist the supplier in understanding the manufacturer's internal needs, designs and specifications. Strategies will be explained to the entire supplier base, focusing initially on the first wave of parts that will be involved. Emphasis is placed on the point that reduction in total number of suppliers means greater volume for those remaining suppliers. The explanation of flow strategies to the supplier includes:

- Involvement in the design process

- Elimination of purchase orders and implementation of quantity releases

- Flexibility requirements and management

- Packaging strategies

- Transportation strategies

- Single-sourcing goals

- Quality at the source techniques

- Demand Flow manufacturing forecasting contracts

- Use of advanced communications

General Strategies

Instead of issuing traditional purchase orders, a DFT contract will be negotiated and requirement releases made against the contract. The supplier and manufacturer will utilize electronic data interchanges through their computer systems to allow simple releases on a frequent basis, with less paperwork, to handle more frequent deliveries. While more frequent deliveries are anticipated, increased product costs are not anticipated or acceptable. Focus will be placed on reducing the quantity of parts in the bill of material and reducing the number of part numbers. If the Demand Flow manufacturer started with 5,000 suppliers, the effort will concentrate on reducing that number to 2,000, then to 500. Packaging will be reviewed and possibly redesigned with an eye toward sizing for RIP quantities and reducing handling damage and costs. Quality parts, on-time delivery and lower costs are the primary objectives. Advanced communications through Electronic Data Interchange (EDI) will be one of the techniques used in achieving lowered costs without an increase in paperwork. Special attention will also be given to transportation networks. Efforts will be made to trim the number of suppliers of the same part and commodity to one preferred supplier.

Why Single-Source Suppliers

Demand Flow manufacturing's emphasis on single-source suppliers should not be confused with the sometimes scary practice, often by regulatory agencies, of using sole-source suppliers. Sole-source suppliers are the only ones in the world that make or supply a particular part. If you want or need that part, you must go to those suppliers on their terms. Single-source suppliers are those selected by the manufacturer or customer to be the exclusive supplier for a particular part. This exclusive selection is the decision of the selection team and buyer, and it is based on several other advantages. The choice of doing business exclusively with one supplier on a particular part is contrary despite the fact that there are other suppliers willing and able to provide the particular part. This choice is contrary to the decision related to using sole-source supplier parts.

Highly Advantageous

There are several advantages to converting to single-source suppliers. In single-sourcing, a supplier is selected and a contract negotiated. Any disadvantages are mitigated by qualifying a second source and factoring in the potential for higher costs by making the investment for quality with the second or backup supplier. It can prove worthwhile to pay tooling costs for a second supplier even if the need to use that supplier is simply not anticipated. Whether or not to qualify a second supplier is a business decision in which added costs must be balanced against possible long lead times and quality problems if problems develop with the single-source supplier. With regard to the single-source supplier, purchased volumes should not amount to more than 30 percent of the supplier's business. An amount greater than 30 percent would put the supplier on shaky ground if the manufacturer's business drops. If such a supplier goes out of business, supply problems for the Demand Flow manufacturer will quickly develop. The exception might be if the manufacturer accounts for more than 30 percent of a company or division of a major corporation.

Better Control/Bigger Slice

The advantages of using a single-source supplier include:

- Being able to focus on that one source

- Consolidating volume

- Consolidating by commodity

- Maintaining better control

- Monitoring of quality and supplier performance

Also, a supplier getting the whole loaf instead of half or a quarter or a slice is much more inclined to keep the buyer happy. The buyer has more time to focus on a smaller number of suppliers and is better able to monitor performance and contract flexibility.

Focus on Total Cost

The emphasis will shift away from the traditional, standard material cost of a purchased item towards the total cost of the part. Other costs in addition to the standard material cost must be considered. Cost of quality, transportation, packaging, setup and carrying inventory are other elements of total cost. It may be that the supplier with the lowest standard cost may not have the lowest total cost due to high rework, scrap or transportation cost.

Initial Focus

Conversion of suppliers to Demand Flow Technology is a gradual and deliberate process. During the inspection of their premises, attention is paid to union affiliations, high customer turnover, all new production employees or a manufacturing process that has had multiple managers in the past six months. The buyer inspects for things that might interrupt the flow of quality goods to his plant. In qualifying and certifying the supplier and its processes, the buyer investigates the financial stability of the supplier, neatness and orderliness of the plant, and plant safety. Questions to be asked include:

- Is there a logical physical flow to their product?

- How does the supplier measure and control the production flow?

- How aware are the employees of current production techniques?

- How do the supplier's financial ratios compare to industry norms?

- How stable is the management team?

- Does the supplier understand process capability techniques?

- Can the supplier prove its process capability statistically and does it understand the variables related to its own process?

As a part of the certification process, pareto analysis and control charts are set up to monitor parts at the supplier; data is sent to the buyer's quality team with a closed-loop corrective action program; and arrangements are made for periodic audits of the supplier's facility, processes and materials. While the supplier will become an extension of the buyer's production process, the buyer's quality development team will become an extension of the supplier's process.

Design Process Modifications

Product design is crucial in seeking *world-class* manufacturing excellence. However, design people traditionally tend to proliferate part numbers. If there are several existing parts that could be used for a new product, designers are likely to create a new one. Often, design engineering does not access the preferred part and supplier databases that allow them to recognize existing preferred part numbers and preferred single-source suppliers. Computer-Aided Design (CAD) tools and the network links to the resident manufacturing system must be available to aid the designer in part standardization and selection.

Supplier Involvement

The supplier should become involved in the design process as early as possible. The Demand Flow manufacturer will give the supplier a preliminary set of purchase specifications that include required and optional dimensions, tolerances and performance attributes. The *required* specifications, attributes, tolerances, materials, processes and costs must be met. Other attributes of a component can have optional parameters in which trade-offs can be offered by the supplier. For example, the supplier can produce a two percent tolerance component utilizing alternate materials for a $10,000 tooling cost, or $0.10 per unit. Or, they can produce a one percent tolerance device utilizing an alternate technology for $0.15 per unit and $100,000 tooling costs. The buyer/engineer can select the appropriate technology depending on the required specification of the device. The Demand Flow manufacturer must be careful that the material is not over specified and that a component that is far better and more costly than what is required to meet product specification is not obtained. Engineering should be encouraged to design existing materials/parts into new products wherever possible. At the conclusion of the discussions among design, purchasing, manufacturing engineering and the supplier, each part specification and attribute should be covered by the agreed-upon specifications. There should be no confusion over the definition of a quality criteria for the part at this point. There can be no "specification disconnect" between buyer expectations and supplier capabilities.

Developing a Contract

Ultimately, a DFT contract will be written for as many different part numbers as possible. Initially, one might select the highest dollar volume part (calculated by multiplying annual usage by unit cost). Once the decision is made on which supplier to go with, a contract is drafted. The qualifying, selecting and contracting process continues with suppliers, part by part. Other considerations affecting the initial priorities for contract selection include:

- Space-intensive parts

- Material with tight quality specifications

- Parts critical to the product

- Parts involving high transportation costs

- Impact of inventory carrying costs

Contract Elements

Several elements are essential to a successful DFT contract. Under the quality provision, the suppliers agree to supply material per specifications, to monitor and control their process as required to ensure compliance to parameters and acceptance criteria, and to share information regarding the control and monitoring of their process. Changes in the supplier's process will be agreed upon in writing if they affect form, fit or function of the item produced. The contract includes:

- Stipulation that all amendments must be in writing

- Description and mutually agreed-upon specifications with reference to critical parameters and acceptance criteria

- Total quantity over the contract life

- Beginning and ending dates of the contract

The shared forecast and flexible lead time are significant elements of the DFT contract.

Negotiated Flexibility and Forecast

A typical DFT contract clause might include provisions such as: "Buyer will provide a rolling forecast equal in length to the buyer's planning horizon, updated monthly with windows for adjusting positive and negative variances to forecasted quantities. Seller's lead time for shipment shall be one week after receipt of the release." This lead time is a consideration only at the outset of the contract. One of the reasons suppliers' lead time is so long in traditional manufacturing is that the suppliers have no real visibility beyond their lead time, since they have no idea what the next purchase order will bring. The Demand Flow manufacturing contract plugs certainty into getting additional business and flexibility into fulfilling it.

Flexibility Grows

Consider a 24-month contract for 1,000,000 parts. The contract would probably call for release of 10,000 per week for the first four weeks before falling into the flexibility time fence: releases of between 9,000 and 11,000 each week for weeks four to nine; releases of between 8,000 and 12,000 each week for weeks nine to thirteen; and releases of between 7,000 and 13,000 thereafter for duration of the contract. If the Demand Flow manufacturers do not utilize the flexibility in the contract, they could wind up with either excess inventory or a major shortage. It may be that the Demand Flow manufacturer's needs would be cut back to the low end of the contract's flexibility, around 7,000, or kick up to 13,000 depending on their actual demands. However, in the absence of other direction, the supplier will continue to ship 10,000 each and every week.

Maintain Flexibility

Marketing and supplier flexibility must be kept in synchronization. In signing the contract, the flow manufacturer does commit to buying a percentage of the 1,000,000 parts over the life of the contract. The commitment is part of the contract; however, two stipulations can ease the situation if business conditions change:

- Provide that the Demand Flow manufacturer can extend the contract for some reasonable time frame in order to consume the contracted quantity;

- Negotiate a conciliation charge if the quantity commitment is not fulfilled.

Release provisions of the contract should stipulate that multiple releases will be made with quantities to be determined, shipping dates, shipping method, carrier, destination, release mode, allowable variances from forecast and the quality requirement windows, and frequency of shipments. Caution should be used to avoid writing DFT contracts for material with only short-term use, or material that is likely to become obsolete. A careful check with design engineering should be made before contract negotiations begin.

Contract Freight

It is essential for the Demand Flow manufacturer to maintain control of shipping. The DFT contract should state that shipping is FOB point of origin and that the buyer will specify shipping method and carrier. The supplier will be liable for incremental costs incurred when an unspecified carrier is used. The buyer should have the right to accept or reject late or early shipments as well as shipments in excess of the release or pull quantity. The supplier should be required to notify the manufacturer of delays immediately and then ship the fastest means with increased cost paid by the supplier. In a flow system it can be just as bad to receive shipments early, which could be dangerous in a RIP inventory system without a storeroom, as it is to receive shipments late.

Inspection

Initially, the Demand Flow manufacturer will inspect the supplier's material when it is received, even with a DFT contract. Depending on the supplier's quality history, it may take a long period of time to become comfortable with the supplier's quality conformance before eliminating inspections. Gradually, the number of inspections decreases and lots are skipped as the effort moves toward complete elimination of incoming inspections. If inspections are eliminated too quickly, the point of discovery for bad parts will be in the in-process product, exposing the Demand Flow manufacturer to increased rework and scrap costs. The DFT contract should stipulate that the Demand Flow manufacturer has the right to inspect the supplier's plant and production process and should define the flow manufacturer's right to randomly audit the supplier's process. Emphasis should be placed on assisting the supplier to establish comprehensive in-process quality techniques at the supplier's location and in the supplier's process rather than inspecting and sorting parts. Initial inspections of the supplier's process may begin at a rate of once every couple of days and gradually decrease to once a month as the supplier's in-process quality improves. It may take a year or more to bring the quality levels to the desirable level, but such inspections are a way to minimize quality problems at the outset and bring the supplier as swiftly as possible to the quality level required.

Recourse for Noncompliance

A point system should be established to provide recourse in the event the supplier fails to meet contract requirements to an appreciable degree. As an example, being early or late on a shipment might be one point. Being early or late on a shipment to the degree that the process is upset might be ten points. With other points assessed on failure to perform on other contract provisions, the contract might give the manufacturer the right to cancel the contract if a level of 30 points is reached in three months.

Invoicing/Price

Important points in creating a DFT contract:

- Mode of invoice, such as written or electronic, plus applicable discounts and best time frame for invoices should be spelled out in the DFT contract.

- A specific price should be quoted for the life of the contract, though the price may be allowed to vary depending on the term. It may not be reasonable to assume that a price can be fixed for the term of a five-year contract, as an example.

• Price separately any operation or process that may potentially be deleted within the term of the contract in order to avoid repricing upon deletion.

• Allow for reductions in the price during the term of the agreement if the seller can realistically be expected to gain economic improvements through continual total quality control of the process.

• Define formulas for indexing against a particular commodity on unique raw material prices.

The approach to allow a price fluctuation further illustrates that in the Demand Flow manufacturing relationship, the supplier is basically an extension of the flow manufacturing plant. If the supplier saves $1 per unit through a joint improvement in the process, the Demand Flow manufacturer should expect to receive a percentage of savings in reduced part costs. If, due to reasons beyond the supplier's control, cost of the unit goes up, the Demand Flow manufacturer expects to share in that increase. There is no interest in beating up the supplier or seeking an unrealistic and arbitrary price reduction for a specified period without assisting in improving the production processes.

Advantages to Supplier

There are many advantages to a flow supplier:

- The suppliers receive a longer forecast or horizon of visibility, which facilitates better planning and reduces their lead time requirements.

- The suppliers also receive frequent releases. Consistent shipments mean consistent cash flow.

- The Demand Flow manufacturer will consolidate invoices to some extent but will still pay the flow manufacturing suppliers quickly. In fact, a promise needs to be made to the suppliers that the manufacturer will not age their invoices.

- Setups occur frequently and become a consistent part of each supplier's process of improving quality and production process.

- Frequent shipments also allow the suppliers to carry less inventory.

- Suppliers receive immediate feedback of quality problems and the need to incorporate process improvements.

- Single-source suppliers receive 100 percent of the manufacturer's business for the particular part or parts involved as well as a long-term strategic relationship.

- Suppliers can better plan materials and plant capacity.

Better Cash Flow

Some of those advantages are particularly clear when applied to different time frames. Consider 1,000 units priced at $100,000 which are required during a four-week period. If the units were shipped every four weeks, cash flows every four weeks, and the quality exposure is on 1,000 units. The supplier and the manufacturer are both required to carry inventory. There may be only one setup every four weeks, a time spread that will not assure process familiarity, setup reduction efficiency or reduced quality exposure. Consider the same usage on a weekly basis. The cash flow is weekly. Maximum quality exposure is 250 units. Maximum inventory carried by either company can be 250 units. Efficient setups can be made weekly versus only once every four weeks.

Transportation Strategy

Apart from the transportation provisions of the contract, cost-effective transportation is a goal of the Demand Flow manufacturer. There may be a greater transportation demand, and the service needs to be better and more dependable, but it is essential that no additional money be spent on reaching that objective. There is no advantage to spending on transportation that which is saved in inventory. These are some measures which should be considered:

- Consolidate shipments geographically to qualify for the lowest rates.

- Replace ordering costs with transportation costs in the parts period balancing formula to optimize costs when volume is not large enough for price breaks.

- Use deregulation of the freight industry and negotiate.

- Consolidate shipments with other companies and, where possible, coordinate trucking back hauls.

- Investigate rail and air modes of transportation. No longer are the trucking companies always the least expensive mode of transportation.

- Consolidate freight volume to minimize costs. If the FOB point is factory, the contract may specify the use of the same carrier for inbound as well as outbound.

- Explore all options and monitor industry regulation changes. Do not award business on price rate alone.

- Award long-term contracts. Negotiate a DFT contract with the transportation company similar to the contract with suppliers. Make sure quality and responsibility for parts damaged in transit are a part of the contract.

Packaging Strategies

Henry Ford is reputed to be the first person to recycle packaging in the United States. The story goes that he bought the engines for his Model T from the Dodge Brothers, and he asked them to drill three holes in specific places on the side of the wooden box used to ship the engines. They complied, and later asked him why. The reason: Henry Ford used that panel of the box as the floorboard in the Model T, and the holes were for the pedals.

Packaging does not always allow for that kind of reuse, but it does provide the opportunity to reward the creative.

As an example, on a particular computer base, negotiations were made with the supplier to ship the base with a specific pallet attached. When the base was received, the pallet was left attached. The product was built on the base, and since the pallet wasn't removed, they traveled through the production process together. Upon completion, the shipping box was attached to the original base and pallet, and the completed unit was shipped in the same container that brought in the base component. That kind of utility eliminates both a trash problem and the cost of additional packaging.

Many Opportunities Presented

Packaging specifications should be called out in the DFT contract.

- The supplier will be required to package material per specified standards with changes agreed upon mutually and in writing.

- Packaging should facilitate handling, counting and storage.

- Packaging should be designed to afford maximum protection to ensure that the quality of the parts remains intact.

- Quantity per package and/or size of package should be set to facilitate delivery to and use at the line in a Kanban quantity.

- Trash problems or recycling should be considered in package design, as should electronic bar coding techniques which may smooth out and speed up receiving.

The objective is to eliminate as many nonvalue-added steps as possible in unpacking, repackaging, counting and processing trash. The design engineer, process engineer and buyer should focus systematically on these topics and eliminate the added costs for these nonvalue-added steps.

Advanced Communication

Ordering costs can be lowered with the advanced communication systems available today. Consider as an example: forecasts and releases are transmitted via a modem; bar codes on incoming packaging are used for receiving material; invoices are transmitted via modem; payment is made by an electronic funds transfer. Speed is enhanced; paperwork is minimized. Even with the elimination of traditional transactions by a Demand Flow manufacturer, there is no better substantiation than that provided by the Demand Flow manufacturing process: if you built the product, you must have had the parts. This topic is further discussed in Chapter 13.

Initial Purchasing Priorities

The Demand Flow production process is well underway before a contract receives any consideration. Before negotiating a DFT contract, priorities in the manufacturing plant include resolving major quality issues and assisting production in becoming linear by producing a 99 percent service level. Once the production process is linear, we can select primary suppliers to begin strategic relationships on the basis of:

- Sole-source parts

- High-dollar parts

- Space-intensive parts

- Critical-specification parts

- Inventory carrying costs

Quality techniques and freight issues rise in importance: define optimal lot size and vary deliveries according to demand; reduce safety stocks as quality and delivery problems are solved.

Second Phase

The second phase of contract negotiations may include:

- Additional packaging improvements, taking the parts directly to RIP

- Electronic invoicing/order release

- Elimination of change orders and communicating releases against contract

- Biweekly deliveries

- Tightening allowable performance points

- Earlier involvement by the supplier in future product design change

Supplier benefits from this include:

- Reduced supplier base, supplier volume increased

- Receiving forecasts each week rather than the previous month, quarter or annual estimate

- Guaranteed quantities

- Improved quantity and delivery performance to a major customer

Example of Savings

One of the renegade divisions of GTE that converted to Demand Flow Technology enjoyed improved delivery service on components while saving $800,000 per year on price and quality improvements. They found defective units caused by a conflict in specifications between them and their supplier. They also found that bringing in components that were stored for several months in a standard cardboard box reduced the solderability of the component's leads. Under the DFT contract, electrostatic discharge sensitive packaging was used for the components and storage time was drastically reduced. The component defect rate went from three percent to 150 parts per million. Price per unit went from $.79 per unit in 1986 to $.65 per unit in 1989 due to a doubling of volume and elimination of secondary suppliers. Supplier quoted lead time was decreased from 20 weeks to four weeks. One supplier received orders for 2,800,000 units rather than three suppliers supplying 933,000 units each. Packaging, inspection and other related process improvements were also made. The bottom line: $400,000 a year savings in price; $200,000 a year savings in rework costs; $200,000 a year savings in incoming inspection costs.

These kinds of savings are not unusual in a flow manufacturer/supplier relationship; other DFT manufacturers have experienced results that dwarf those in this GTE example.

Changing Role of Demand Flow Manufacturing Buyer

Today's traditional buyers spend most of their time on order launching and expediting. This includes: reviewing the requirements for purchased material, determining which of several qualified suppliers the order will be placed with, phoning the supplier for confirmation, mailing a purchase order document, and following up to ensure on-time delivery (or postmortem to find out why it was late). Typically, the original due date of the purchase order with its long lead time will vary significantly from the actual "need date" of the purchase order. After navigating multiple planning cycles, which can vary the due date of the purchase order, today's buyer struggles to keep up with the "pull ins" and often has no time for the "push outs." Material planning reports and traditional management reports have proliferated. Each time a planning cycle occurs, the traditional MRP II computer system recalculates all existing required dates and provides messages on how to reschedule existing purchase orders.

Process Gyrations

Because the traditional planning cycle can vary requirements so wildly, purchase order due dates "bounce" from one date to another. This creates havoc for the buyer attempting to manage this process and for the supplier attempting to keep up with this shifting. Often, buyers have so many messages due to the planning system sensitivity that they cannot keep up.

Also, the traditional relationship between what is actually required on the production floor and the MRP II reports is somewhat tenuous. For example, six work orders or kits of parts in staging, requiring a quantity of six of the same part numbers, can't be released with just one part being received. All six are needed. All material, once allocated to the six work orders, is frozen, and that material cannot be used on other products. It can be very confusing to the buyer to determine what is actually required to "keep production going." Buyers often revert to the manual system of using "Hot Lists" generated by manufacturing.

Purchase Orders Costly

The material that the traditional buyer procures has specific purchase order line-item identity, quantities and delivery date definition. The average cost of creating a purchase order ranges from $50 to $200 each, depending on the company. This includes paperwork, postage and handling, clerical and buyer's time. It does not include expediting, quality or shortage costs. Since the cost of the purchase order is so high, traditional buyers tend to group or "lot size" material requirements and buy bigger batches to minimize the purchase order ordering costs. The formula by which traditional manufacturers tend to balance inventory carrying costs and purchase order placement cost is known as "Part Period Balancing" (P.P.B.). For example, if part number 17203 had a purchase order cost of $100 and average inventory of 1,000 units, it would incur a standard cost of $1 and 30 percent inventory carrying cost per year. The following would be indicated:

$$\frac{Procurement\ Cycle}{(P.P.B.)} = \frac{30\% \ x \ 1{,}000 \ x \ \$1}{\$100} = 3$$

Order/Purchase Order Cost = $100

Inventory Carrying Cost Per Year = 30%

1,000 (ave. inv.) x $1 (unit cost) = $1,000

The figure indicates that the part should be purchased three times a year. The most the part could be turned would be three times a year since it is being purchased in four-month quantities. The problem with the traditional part period balancing formula is that the order cost per purchase order is used for a basis to calculate how often to buy the part. If the cost of ordering were incurred only once a year and deliveries were managed on a more frequent basis, the inventory could be turned on a more frequent basis without incurring additional overhead. This is the objective of the DFT buyer.

It is highly recommended that DFT buyers should plan as well as buy their own material. Material planning, through the single-level bill of material explosion, will indicate to the buyer whether flexibility to the negotiated plan needs to be exercised. If marketing has increased the forecast, purchasing must advise the supplier that additional requirements within the flexibility parameters are needed. As an example:

Product: Model-797X

Negotiated Level: 100/week

Purchased Part: 921317-01

Quantity Per on Bill of Material: 1

Delivery Cycle: Weekly (currently 100/week)

Marketing has indicated a desire to increase Model-797X to 120/week beginning in week six, which is within the negotiated flex fences. Material planning would indicate:

	wk 1	wk 2	wk 3	wk 4	wk 5	wk 6	wk 7	wk 8
Part Number: Model-797X								
Gross Requirement	100	100	100	100	100	120	120	120
Scheduled Receipts								
On Hand	0	0	0	0	0	0	0	0
Net Requirements	100	100	100	100	100	120	120	120
Part Number: 921317-01								
Gross Requirement	100	100	100	100	100	120	120	120
Scheduled Receipts	100	100	100	100	100	100	100	100
On Hand	0	0	0	0	0	0	0	0
Net Requirements	0	0	0	0	0	20	20	20

Scheduled receipts would be obtained from the delivery schedule in the DFT contract. The contract would indicate the normal delivery in the scheduled receipts. Negotiated flexibility to scheduled deliveries would be indicated in net requirements. It would be indicated to the supplier, preferably electronically, that beginning in week six, 20 additional units, totalling 120 units, will be needed. No offset of the supplier requirements is necessary if the requested flexibility is within the negotiated contract parameters.

A decision may be made by the buyer to carry some additional inventory temporarily to cover quality, delivery or other problems. This inventory may also be used to cover marketing flexibility requirements that exceed the capability of their suppliers. For example, assume the buyer is required to keep an additional 10 percent inventory on a critical part that is difficult to forecast. Using the previous example, the material plan would indicate:

	wk 1	wk 2	wk 3	wk 4	wk 5	wk 6	wk 7	wk 8
Part Number: Model-797X								
Gross Requirement	100	100	100	100	100	120	120	120
Scheduled Receipts								
On Hand	0	0	0	0	0	0	0	0
Net Requirements	100	100	100	100	100	120	120	120
Part Number: 921317-01								
Gross Requirement	100	100	100	100	100	120	120	120
Scheduled Receipts	110	110	110	110	110	110	110	110
On Hand	10	20	30	40	50	40	30	20
Net Requirements	0	0	0	0	0	0	0	0

The buyer has been able to cover up to six additional weeks of the increase without exercising the material flexibility of the contract. This may be an effective, although expensive, preferred strategy on low-dollar and low-volume parts. Traditional safety-stock quantities should not be netted out in advance of the material planning but should remain visible as it is focused on and eliminated.

Demand Flow Manufacturing
Initial Purchasing Goals

The buyer should focus on getting parts on DFT contracts and then managing flexibility. An initial goal of Demand Flow manufacturing purchasing should be to get 70 percent of Class A parts on a DFT flexible contract. This would mean that only a small percentage of part numbers would be on a DFT flexible contract initially; however, over half of the annual investment in material would be positively impacted. As the Demand Flow Technology implementation progresses, Class B parts can be scrutinized and the focus applied to placing them on a commodity contract consolidation.

If a company has 1,000 purchased active parts, the initial goal should be to have 35 Class A parts on contract by the end of the first phase. These parts should be the ones which are tied to the processes being converted to Demand Flow manufacturing. Daily deliveries can be called out after 90 percent-plus manufacturing linearity has been obtained.

The DFT buyer should also obtain contracts for transportation and work towards setting up freight networks. The buyer's goal will be to increase the number of deliveries without increasing transportation costs. Inexpensive Class C items may be delivered on an infrequent basis. Here, the part period balancing formula may be utilized to determine frequency of delivery. As transportation costs are reduced, delivery frequency may be increased. As an example:

Day 1

Transportation Cost/Delivery: $50

Inventory Carrying Cost: $1 (std. cost) x 30%
(ICC)

Usage = 100/week or $30

A weekly delivery would cost more per week ($50) than the cost of holding the inventory ($30). Bimonthly deliveries will become appropriate as the transportation costs are driven downward through networking and single-source transportation. Eventually, weekly deliveries may become appropriate. Buyers, with the aid of the computer, need to manage the delivery cycle with a focus on total cost.

Demand Flow Manufacturing Buyer Evolution

Traditional manufacturing buyers spend about 75 percent of their time in order launching and expediting. The remaining 25 percent of their time is devoted to clerical functions, negotiating price, keeping production going, managing by report, rescheduling deliveries in and out, and attending Material Review Board (MRB) meetings. The buyer in Demand Flow manufacturing evolves into: managing flexibility; Kanban management and pre-shortage analysis; deep involvement in DFT flexible contracts; transportation, packaging and supplier management; planning as well as buying material with total cost emphasis; and assisting in getting the process linear. They can have a positive impact on the total cost of a product. Their objectives should include a two to three percent material cost reduction per year through the use of flow techniques applied to their supplier base and through the education and assistance of their new "team" members.

Chapter Nine

Total Employee Involvement

Why become a *world-class* manufacturer? What is the purpose? Aren't other manufacturing technologies or philosophies acceptable? Global reasons for converting to *world-class* Demand Flow manufacturing technology are outlined in the beginning of this book. Company reasons for implementing Demand Flow manufacturing are simple:

- Customer responsiveness

- Quality improvement

- Overall cost reduction

- Survival

Actually, some American companies are becoming proficient at reducing costs. However, many of those cost reductions were obtained through an arbitrary percentage that must be cut to maintain profitability rather than through productivity, quality or process improvements. Demand Flow manufacturing cost reductions are true improvements. Expected improvements in cost can be substantial and dramatic. Demand Flow manufacturing results can be as impressive as the following actual statistics:

CATEGORY	Company A	Company B
WIP Dollars	Down 70%	Down 80%
Floor Space	Down 30%	Down 52%
Scrap/Rework Cost	Down 44%	Down 35%
Mfg. Output = People	Up 16%	Up 20%
Labor Efficiency	Up 26%	Up 31%
Inventory Turnover	From 3 to 24	7 to 41
Cycle Time	From 8 weeks to 52 minutes	From 4 weeks to 40 minutes

These results or goals are achievable for the manufacturer who implements Demand Flow Technology in an organized, uncompromising manner. Demand Flow manufacturing should never be sold as a work force reduction program. While it is true that the Demand Flow manufacturer will require a significantly smaller number of resources in some areas, other areas will require more resources. Due to Demand Flow manufacturing improvements, the Demand Flow manufacturer will produce higher quality and lower cost products to entice marketing to sell more products that the same work force can support without an increase. Retirement and attrition will take care of any work force adjustments. Support of the DFT implementation program from all levels is mandatory for the implementation to be successful. Ways of utilizing the work force, freed up from traditional functions, must be examined as part of the implementation process.

Economic Survival

Many companies began converting to Demand Flow manufacturing in the 1980s. The trend has increased substantially throughout the 1990s and will continue into the 21st century. The reason is economic survival for the companies and the United States' economy. Much has been made of the 19 million jobs created in a previous federal administration. However, some 88 percent of those jobs were in the service sector of the economy. Such jobs do not create wealth and, in the longterm, will not sustain the standard of living in the United States. The number of manufacturing jobs in the United States continues to erode. The difference between the pay of a created job and a lost job is an average of between $10,000 and $21,500 less. The United States economy is creating lower-paying, service-sector jobs, and losing higher-paying, manufacturing-sector jobs. This pattern is expected to continue. Federal and trade deficits continue to grow, partially as a result of this trend. Improvements reported recently must be carefully filtered to segregate current phenomena from actual productivity improvements. In order to survive and to grow, the United States manufacturing industry must improve. Demand Flow manufacturing is the technology and foundation that can fully support that improvement.

Most Important Asset

As manufacturing technology evolves from the traditional, labor tracking, scheduling, batch mentality to the Demand Flow Technology, the way in which people are involved in the technology changes as well. People are the most important asset of any company. In a Demand Flow manufacturing environment, the responsibilities and work content of many employees change. As the roles change, the organizations to support the people tend to change. In traditional manufacturing, people are told what to do and how to do it.

Communication Failures

The traditional manufacturing company consists of many layers or levels of management. Information, goals, expectations and philosophies tend to get translated as information gets passed down through the various levels. The phenomenon is rarely intentional, but each level brings a unique perspective to events and a unique interpretation of information. By the time the information reaches the people or the level for which it was originally intended, it may bear little resemblance to the initial message. Direct exposure of the lower tiers of the organization to the upper echelon of the company is infrequent and formal in nature.

Furthermore, information passed from the bottom up through the levels of the organization suffers the same fate. Middle-level managers typically do not want to bother higher levels with details and information from the ranks. The information becomes more heavily summarized as it gets passed up. The information also suffers from a phenomenon known as "filtering" in which information detrimental to the middle levels is hidden or buried in statistical gobbledegook. This is human nature, but it makes getting the proper information to the proper decision maker in a timely fashion very difficult.

Surpassing Level of Competence

Another phenomenon typical to American manufacturing is the "Peter Principle," which states that a person will be promoted to the level of his or her incompetence. Management positions are highly valued in our country for economic and status reasons. An individual may be an excellent engineer, even though he or she has not received sufficient training or experience to become a manager of engineers. The individual desires the promotion and must break into management in order to progress and receive increased compensation. When the individual's goal has been achieved, when the inevitable promotion comes, net effect to the company is the loss of a good engineer and the gain of an inexperienced manager. In DFT, the reward systems for both direct and salaried employees must change.

Maligned Employees Not the Problem

Production employees in the United States have been battered and maligned in the last several years. They are accused of being the cause of the decline of manufacturing in this country due to the high demand for wages and other compensation, often through unions. At the same time, there have been reports of loss of productivity or lack of productivity improvement, further contributing to the loss of jobs. Compounding the assault on American production employees is the cry that quality of workmanship has severely diminished in recent years. Although the root of deteriorating American manufacturing appears obvious, it is not. An examination of the underlying causes will reveal that the root of the problem is in management practices, organizations and compensation strategies.

There has been a flood of books, articles and consultants on organizational development, management styles and theories dealing with people and various other human resource topics. As American companies attempt to compete and to survive, several things become clear:

Flexibility, Participation Come of Age

- Flexibility is a valued skill in a company. The age of specialization is over. No longer can the work force focus on a narrow range of skills. The markets and companies are changing too quickly.

- Participative management is a concept whose time has come. As organizations become leaner in an effort to remain competitive, they must utilize the resources that are available. They need to harness the creative problem-solving abilities of the work force, as well as to utilize technical and administrative skills. Participative management is the ability to participate, in advance of implementation, in making decisions by those people whose responsibilities will be affected by the decisions.

Involvement, Compensation Change

- Employee involvement must become an ingrained part of the manufacturing culture, an integral part of a company's way of doing business. A giant leap of faith must be taken and the assumption made that the person who best knows how to do and improve an operation is the person actually doing it. It is essential not only to get input from the operator but to act upon that input as well. Often, the launch of an employee involvement program is followed by a flood of employee recommendations, many of which are not investigated. Employees become disillusioned and stop participating. In most cases, a nonexistent employee involvement program is better than a non-supported employee involvement program.

- Compensation programs must be modified to meet the changing responsibilities and organization shifts that are occurring. Pay must be tied to flexibility, team and organizational performance, employee involvement, participation and resultant improvements. The seniority, pay for title or position-based pay programs, common in industry today, will not survive the competitive requirements and changing technologies.

People Make a Difference

In the 1980s, the Ford Motor Company did a $6.3 billion turnaround. The company went from an annual loss of $3.1 billion at the beginning of the decade to a profit of $3.2 billion in 1987. When asked to what he attributed the dramatic turnaround, Ford's chairman, Donald Peterson, said a primary reason was people—participative management and employee involvement. He defined employee involvement as "the soliciting of input of the employees on how to improve the process, and taking action on that input."

World-class manufacturing is accomplished through people—people play a more dramatic, extensive and critical role than in traditional manufacturing methods. Employees get more training and do more, different operations—they have more, different responsibilities. That is why they are called flexible employees. They are paid for their flexibility rather than their seniority. Production employees are responsible for quality, and, unlike in traditional scheduled manufacturing, the production employees can stop the line. Production employees can be trainees and trainers—they can move to leadership positions or to replenishing the Kanbans if a material handler does not come around.

Minimum One-Up and One-Down

Production employees in Demand Flow manufacturing must be able to work "one-up" and "one-down"—that is a minimum. They must be able to do the operation on either side of them; they must be able to do at least three different operations: their own, the one immediately before it in the process, and the one immediately after it in the process or cell. An employee at the beginning of a process must learn one position up and the operation of the immediately preceding process; an employee at the end of the process, in addition to learning one position down, must learn the next operation in the next process or that of material handling.

If a production employee reaches for a unit to work on and there is no unit there, that employee moves in the direction of the pull, to work on a unit to supply the empty station. The employees are not told to do this—it is an automatic response to the absence of units flowing to their station. Employees can help complete the units flowing to their station and then return to their station, or the next operator down the line will move down and take position in the then vacant station. The process and movement of employees is that simple: an employee goes to pull a unit, there's nothing there, the employee moves in the direction of pull.

Greater Production Flexibility

That is in marked contrast to traditional manufacturing in which, if no product were there, the employees would remain at their idled positions and perhaps make a report of the situation. If fewer people are in the process, although the work content is not changed, the observed operational cycle time increases. Due to employee flexibility in the Demand Flow manufacturing system, this is a process that can run with 50 percent of the employees absent. Although the observed cycle time will increase and the volume of products will decrease proportionally, the Demand Flow manufacturing process can run smoothly if every other employee is absent. Conversely, if there is a need to produce fewer products, employees can be pulled and the process will balance itself. In high turnover situations, one-up, one-down is even more beneficial. No matter how many holes in the process must be plugged by the flexible employees, verification and total quality control are still performed and work content does not change. One-up, one-down is the minimum requirement to work in a Demand Flow manufacturing process. Once this is attained, the employee may decide to reach further flexibility standards, such as two-up, two-down, three-up, three-down, and so forth. Eventually, certification in all process operations may be reached by a few employees while others choose to stay at the minimum level of one-up, one-down. Employees usually pursue flexibility horizontally and vertically, e.g., doing several different assembly operations and doing assembly, testing and machine troubleshooting.

Pay for Skill

Employees are paid on the basis of individual flexibility, individual employee involvement, knowledge, skill and teamwork. These, in turn, prompt major changes in the operation of the human resources department. Significantly, an employee is paid for the knowledge of an operation that he or she knows but may not perform daily. Points are applied to different operations (positions). An employee can be: training in a position; certified in a position to do the work without assistance or additional training; or a master in a position, one who has reached the highest level in that position, one with a long period of quality work who can train others for it. Although one-up and one-down represents the minimum requirement, many employees achieve more. It is not unusual for an employee to be a master in a few positions and certified in a few other positions. With points varying per position, depending on the type of work content at the operation, and increasing from trainee to certified to master, it is not unusual for a heavily cross-trained and widely skilled employee to have higher pay than that of the team leader.

Pay Programs

There are four elements of pay in a DFT program:

1. Base wage

2. Flexibility skill points

3. Team and organizational incentives

4. Compensation for employee involvement program activities

The base wage of an employee is based upon existing market value for a given position in the area of the country in which the plant is located. This base wage is an average market value of any particular skill. For example, in California the market value of a production operator position may be $10 per hour, while in Mississippi it may be $4 per hour. Typically, employees will be brought into the Demand Flow manufacturing environment at 80 to 90 percent of market value for base pay. Yearly cost of living adjustments may be applied to the base. This base pay may be anywhere from 50 to 100 percent of an employee's total compensation package. A new employee being hired into the plant will therefore begin with less pay than a similar position in a traditional environment. If the new employee objects to this, he or she is probably not the type of employee preferred for the Demand Flow manufacturing environment. The upside potential with the combination of individual, team and organizational incentives will always be higher in a Demand Flow manufacturing environment. Labor costs, the smallest element of total product cost, may rise somewhat per employee, but it will be offset by the fact that the Demand Flow manufacturing process will require fewer employees. This reduction in labor costs will be overshadowed by decreases in material and other overhead costs, the predominant product cost elements.

Flexibility

After an initial training period, all employees in a DFT environment will be required to be certified in a minimum of three positions. Employees must know their primary positions plus one position up and one position down from the primary. This is required for several reasons. Since employees must verify the previous work content sent to them, they must be familiar with the work content of those positions. They must also be aware of the following position's work content, where that operator will verify their work. Also, management will run various flow lines at different rates. Employees will be inserted or pulled out of a line based upon the current rate of the lines. Each employee does the work and quality defined by the operational method sheets in that operation. As rates decrease, people may be removed and machines turned off, but the designed work content and quality criteria at each operation does not change.

Employees Flow to Need

Flexible employees allow management to adjust the volume of products being produced without changing the operational work or quality criteria of an operation and move to alternate operations without mass retraining efforts. The pull process requires flexible employees. Flexible employees are allowed to fill their in-process Kanban and complete the unit at their station or machine. At this point, their demand is satisfied and they must move downstream. They will then assist at that position until a unit is completed at the downstream operation. The flow line naturally rebalances with flexible employees. Employees must be able to perform upstream and downstream operations in order to make the pull process effective. After the basic requirement of one-up and one-down is met, additional flexibility of the employee should be encouraged and incentives provided. A cap may be placed on the maximum number of operations in which an employee can become certified. Since flexible employees are required to rotate frequently through certified operations, this cap is whatever reasonable number of operations an employee can be expected to work in over a given period of time. After employees have reached the cap on the number of operations of certification, they may increase their pay for skill points via certifying in more difficult tasks (while losing certification in simpler tasks), or becoming team leader (reference Figure 9-1).

Team Incentives

A TQC process team is expected to produce total quality units in a linear fashion. Each process team's linearity index of TQC units will be measured against the daily rate. Team passes, or two operational passes, of nonquality units will be subtracted, as will an overproduction or underproduction, from the daily rate. A linearity goal for each process will be set. A team incentive will be provided for the attainment of that goal. As the process matures, the goal of TQC units will approach the daily rate. Once 97 to 98 percent linearity against the daily rate of TQC units has been obtained, higher team incentives may be awarded. The greater number of "support" people placed on the team incentive plan, such as engineering or quality staff, the better. This fosters a team atmosphere and envelops the support team in the production process focus.

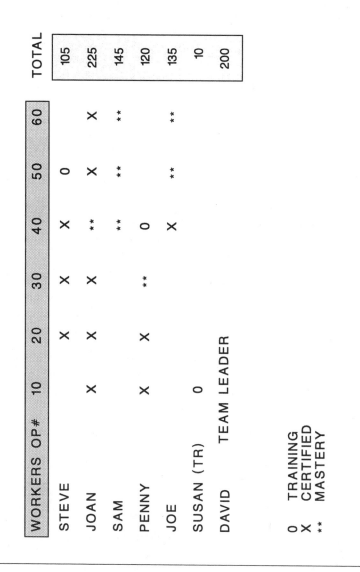

Figure 9-1 Flexible Pay Program

Profit and Joint Sharing

Profit sharing and gain share programs are becoming popular means of associating pay to organizational performance. A key element to these programs is employees providing a portion of their compensation "at risk" against potential sharing of company profits. Typically, a portion of the employee's compensation, usually 5 to 10 percent is put "at risk." If an organization or division achieves less than 80 percent of its profit goals, this "at risk" component is not paid. If between 80 percent and 100 percent of profit goals are obtained, a portion of the "at risk" element is paid out. If profit goals exceeding budgeted levels are attained, then the company has a pot of unexpected "found money." This money is then divided between the company and the employees in some acceptable fashion. Thus, employees' pay is directly tied to organizational performance. In down business cycles, the employees are asked to share in the hardship. While loss of some pay can be difficult, it is often a preferable solution to layoffs or facility closures and consolidation. In profitable times, the employees share in the reward they helped to create. Properly administered, these programs can be powerful motivational and team building tools.

Employee Involvement

The final element of the pay program is tied to participation in the employee involvement program. This will differ from the traditional "suggestion" program in several respects. First, there will be a formal response process imbedded into the program.

A nonexistent employee involvement program is better than a nonresponsive one. Employees will make process improvement suggestions frequently and fervently if they feel valued and if they feel their suggestions will be taken seriously. Often, suggestion programs flounder because resources are not available to respond to suggestions. The biggest impact is typically on design and manufacturing engineering. Suggestions should go above the identify problem/gather data/isolate root causes/monitor solution steps. The suggestions should be made in a team rather than individual mode. Teams should have incentive to make suggestions, not necessarily to find solutions. And, the more "support" functions imbedded in the team, the greater the success.

Typical Demand Flow Manufacturing Pay Program

Job: Production Assembly Employee

Certification Level Job Band: 4

Job Band Rate: $1,500 per month

Market Value: $1,750 per month

Flexibility Factor: Pay for skill point ranges described below

Pay for Skill Ranges

0 - 100 points:	base pay
101 - 150 points:	base plus 10%
151 - 200 points:	base plus 20%
201 - 250 points:	base plus 30%(team leader)

251 - 300 points: base plus 40%(cap)

Team Incentive: 1% for 75 - 80% linearity; 2% for 81 - 90% linearity; 3% for 91 - 95% linearity; 4% for 95 - 98% linearity; 5% for linearity above 98%.

Organizational Incentive: 6% of base at risk; 6% lost at <80%; 1 - 6% paid based on 81 - 100% attainment; over 100%, 50-50 distribution of found money.

For purposes of illustration, Cheryl Baker is a TQC employee in the process. She has attained 180 flexibility points. Her process has averaged 84 percent linearity over the last three months. During the past year, the organization/division has exceeded its profitability goals and has a found money "pot" of $200,000. Some 200 people are in this organization. Cheryl would be paid as follows:

* $1,500 base plus $300 additional flex pay each month;

* Team Incentive: $30 per week bonus for 84 percent linearity (2 percent of $1,500), paid quarterly, $375;

* Organizational Incentive: 50 percent division of found money ($200,000), $100,000 in employee pool divided by 200 employees equals $500 paid annually (this could be scaled based upon earnings);

* Employee Involvement: Cheryl has made 46 process improvement suggestions. Based upon the total number of suggestions and the total savings received by the company, employee share of the savings is equal to $2,000, which is paid quarterly.

As compared with a traditional package of $21,000, Cheryl's total annual compensation package is $25,600 broken down as follows:

- Base $18,000

- Flexibility $3,600

- Team Incentive $1,500

- Organizational Incentive $500

- Employee Involvement $2,000

Direct labor as portion of product cost: 5%

Savings to company: $100,000 found money compensation; benefit dollars from the suggestion savings; intangibles for flexible employee and linearity obtainment.

Administration of such a program is not a minor detail, but can be minimized by consolidating payments and ranging flex values. Was it worth the trouble? Yes, by many tens of thousands of dollars and greater employee satisfaction.

Certification and Mastery Criteria

Certification criteria for a position must be clearly defined. This criteria must include technical work content, educational requirements, quality expectations and the maximum amount of time that can pass between assignments at that position. A "position" is a combination of events that have been grouped together based upon the targeted cycle time of the flow process. A position is not each and every sequence of events in a process, but a grouping of the sequences. One-up, one-down positions may be within what is defined as a "job" for job banding. A team of production, quality, engineering and human resource people will perform the "job banding" function and create the certification criteria one time. Some "jobs" or positional criteria may change over time, and a system needs to be put in place to modify the bands or criteria.

Mastery criteria is based upon two differentials from certification criteria: the production of high-quality parts for a proven period of time, and the ability to train and certify others. Some employees may be fine at a particular craft but couldn't train fish to swim. They will stay at the certification level. For those who wish to attain mastery level at an operation, the company must provide an adequate training program—to "train the trainers."

Sample Certification Criteria

Job Band: #14

Job Description: PCB Assembly

Process/Line: Through hole assembly process

Job Content: Assemble through hole components into PCBs. Verify previous operator's work content. Check TQC points as indicated on method sheet. Ability to operate "contact system" or "manusert" machines. Ability to solder components onto board after insertion.

One-Up/One-Down Operations: Wave solder operation

Minimum Rotation Cycle: Touch-up operation once every four days

Job Value:

Training - 10

Certification - 30

Mastery - 40

Quality Requirements: Maintain process capability of less than 50 parts per million. Maintain operational pareto of position. Two operational passes of less than one per week. Contributed first pass yield at an in-circuit test operation of 99 percent or above.

Once certification criteria is clearly defined, the obtainment of this criteria should be made available to all employees in that process. Training programs should be developed to enable employees to reach higher levels of flexibility. After-hours classes can be offered to the employees to further increase their flexibility, particularly of the vertical variety. This may enable today's production employees to learn through their own initiative, preventative maintenance or test-tech skills that can someday increase their value to the process and increase their pay as well.

Employees may become decertified in a process due to failure to meet called-out criteria, most likely not working in a position often enough to maintain certification. This decertification process is palatable to the employees if they feel they have control over where they work. If opportunities are not given to exercise flexibility and decertification occurs, the employee will feel that it is an unfair action. The determination of who works where and when is a duty of the team leader who needs to be aware of minimum certification requirements and rotation intervals.

Seniority/Unions/Training

Demand Flow Technology does not impact or attempt to impact the seniority position established by employees before conversion. Once conversion is made to DFT, the senior employee will retain the compensation achieved to that point. However, no employee will ride to the top on longevity alone.

If senior employees do not cross-train and achieve mastery, their pay will not increase.

Several unions have embraced DFT for the same reason that employees like it: it gives employees the opportunity to control their own destiny.

While the average annual training expenditure per manufacturing employee in the United States is around $100, the amount required for the *world-class* manufacturer may be much higher. New hires in DFT operations are screened on the basis of adaptability to the flexible TQC process. Marginal employees carried over from traditional manufacturing may find pressure to achieve a level of quality and flexibility proficiency not previously required of them.

Three-Phase Training

An active training program is essential to enable employees to attain and maintain flexibility. The first phase consists of the nontechnical training required for working in the process. The quality department will provide pareto and process control training. Human resources will provide team, employee involvement, effective meeting and interpersonal skill training. Employees will be provided information on the company, its products, customers, values and missions. This phase is a continuous one provided to all employees. It seeks to eliminate one of the shortcomings of traditional manufacturing where employees who help assemble a product have no idea what the finished product looks like and are unfamiliar with the company's goals. This effort is a part of the team building process and, as such, is quite important. For the new employee or during conversion, 40 to 80 hours of this "socio" type training will be provided over the first three to six months of employment or conversion. "State of the company" presentations should also be given quarterly by upper management to all employees in an open and frank manner with adequate time for questions and feedback.

The second phase of training is off-line, where employees are taught basic production skills in an off-line but simulated production environment. Verification and TQC recognition from method sheets are also taught. Usually three days to two weeks of off-line training are provided.

On-line Training Emphasized

The third phase of training is on-line training of a trainee by an experienced employee. The trainee will work in the process with an employee who has obtained a mastery level. The trainee may actually perform the work under the guidance and scrutiny of the skilled employee. The employee at the mastery level is responsible for the quality of the work being performed. During this phase, the trainee will become familiar with the certification criteria for the operation. This certification criteria will include both the technical aspects of the operation, quality criteria and how often an employee must perform the function in order to achieve and maintain certification levels.

Management Structure Changes

All employees become members of a flexible, multitask process with emphasis on better quality and problem solving. *World-class* companies, in terms of management and employees, move from the traditional toward the participatory. There is a blending and perhaps even humbling of roles as the personnel mix of groups change. As an example, the traditional structuring of a manufacturing organization may have included the following: a president and general manager with three vice presidents. The vice president for operations would have under his auspices the manufacturing manager, material manager, manufacturing engineering, quality inspection and testing. The vice president for finance would have the accounting manager, data processing, human resources and office services. The vice president of development would include the engineering manager, technical services, documentation services, and research.

The same company in Demand Flow manufacturing would have a president/general manager and specific product managers. The makeup of staff under each product manager would be basically the same and would include the following:

- Demand-Based Planning

- Purchasing

- Production

- Manufacturing Engineering

- Design Engineering

- Quality

- Accounting/Finance

- DFT Manufacturing Systems

- Maintenance

Team Leader

The team leader is one usually skilled throughout the process who can work in the process when or where needed. Team leaders interface with other team leaders; monitor rate, quality and training; mobilize support functions; and generally manage the process. If there is a particular need, such as for design engineering, the team leader secures it. Team leaders are usually rotated with other production employees. The team leader has many functions, similar to the production superintendent in traditional manufacturing, and the production superintendent's position gives way to the team management of flow manufacturing. Layers of management and interdepartmental politics decrease significantly from traditional manufacturing.

Team Management System

Different teams cover particular areas of the process. They revolve around two central teams: the team management system (TMS) team, which consists of all team leaders; and the global support team, which includes those outside the process, such as suppliers and marketing. TMS and global support are tied under the plant manager. Support members are a part of a production oriented team. Improvement of quality is the immediate objective; improvement of the bottom line is anticipated within two or three years.

Team Objectives

Team leadership is a commitment to training, better work coverage, decreased communications breakdown, higher employee morale, shared risk, and giving individuals more of a direct impact on their income. The professional status of some is lessened, as, for example, a senior staff engineer becomes a part of a team. There are no functional boundaries to serve as obstacles. Career paths and roles may change. A person without a degree may wind up supervising someone with a master's degree. The new mix and increased flexibility means that others can enjoy increased pay and stature under their own control.

New Management/Employee Participation

Management style worldwide is evolving from traditional to participatory with a few companies going even further to a form of socio-production. Traditional management, the method that was virtually universal for most of this century, is completely inflexible: people are told what to do; they are told how to do it. More and more companies are moving toward participatory style which involves job sharing, cross-training and flexibility: employees are told what needs to be done; the team figures out how to do it. In socio-production, the team decides

what to do and how to do it. It is the extreme, and its practice
is rare.

Tradition Yields to Participation

On a scale of one to five, traditional style would be one,
participatory would be three, and socio-production would be
five for such factors as task assignments, operation design,
performance maintenance, organizational design, decision
making, staffing, leadership, compensation, financial controls,
training, technology and people. Specific differences are great
and many. In traditional, people are accountable for their own
work; in participatory they are accountable for their own work
and the work of the team; in socio-production they are comfortable with ambiguity and change. Some companies are more
inclined toward participatory and even socio-production in
some areas while staying near traditional in others.

Demand Flow Technology and
Participatory Management

There is some confusion about the relationship between
Demand Flow Technology and participatory management.
Some executives believe that when they enter participatory
management, they have become a *world-class* Demand Flow
manufacturer. That is not true. Participatory management is one
part of *world-class* Demand Flow manufacturing; DFT is not a
part of participatory management. Participatory management is
a slice of the DFT pie—it is one of the techniques used to

implement Demand Flow Technology. Companies managed in the participatory style are just that; they are not DFT unless they have implemented all other Demand Flow manufacturing techniques as well. The DFT participatory organization with its flexible employees and operational decision making evolves to a flat management structure with teams empowered to make decisions.

Employees Key

The attention to establishing flexible employees is essential in a DFT environment. Flexible employees are key to successful *world-class* Demand Flow manufacturing goals. The compensation systems are changed to reflect the requirements of the Demand Flow Technology. Traditional "job description" classifications with fixed reward systems are outdated and offer little encouragement for individuals to achieve their personal best. Pay systems should be changed when the traditional lines are redesigned for the flow process. In Demand Flow manufacturing, employees are key to the success of the TQC production process.

Chapter Ten

Total Quality Control

D emand Flow manufacturing has a total quality focus that is unbending in its objective of manufacturing excellence. The focus on quality ahead of production is demanded by the customer and is made feasible by the enormous savings in scrap and reworked materials as well as a reduction in overhead costs. Demand Flow manufacturing cannot be achieved without TQC, and TQC cannot be implemented without an effective employee involvement program and a consistent flow process. Who knows the real work content of an operation better than the person performing the work on a day-to-day basis? In a *world-class* Demand Flow process, employees will be stimulated and given incentive to strive toward a goal of total quality and continuous process improvement. An effective employee involvement program must be responsive in order to be effective. While it may not be possible to implement all employee suggestions immediately, and, indeed, many may not appear, on the surface, to be critical to pursue, the employees must feel that they are valued members of the team and that their suggestions are being given due consideration. The greatest cause of failure of employee involvement programs is lack of responsiveness on the part of management and support teams.

TQC in the Process

Total quality control is based upon internal process control at the source of the work. Enforced problem solving is a program that uses all employees, including finance and marketing in addition to materials, engineering, production and quality. All employees in the company will be assigned to an employee involvement team. They may not regularly attend meetings, but they will be on the team and will function at one time or another to improve the process. People from the same support department are put on different quality teams. Any individual or organization may be assigned an action item to respond to from the employee involvement process. The goal is to eliminate organizational partitions and boundaries that are limiting process improvement. Top management participation is mandatory.

A Streamlined Approach

Teams meet only for specific purposes—they go after specific opportunities or problems. They monitor the process, identify problems, isolate root causes, and eliminate those causes. The focus is on process perfection, quality improvement, and cost reduction. The *world-class* company focuses on high quality, process efficiency, elimination of nonvalue-added work in order to lower production cost, total employee involvement and increased customer responsiveness and satisfaction. And, it is all done with a common technology that utilizes the company's people. TQC determines customer expectations, establishes target values, defines process sequence and elements, determines process capabilities, and reduces process variables.

In-Process Quality

The Demand Flow manufacturing methodology of total quality control seeks to eliminate the opportunity to produce a nonquality part, process or product. That effort is made largely through the initial design of the TQC operations and the involvement of people working on quality in the process. In traditional schedulized manufacturing there are a few nonproductive quality determination actions performed by inspectors. In the DFT total quality flow process there are many quality checks and verifications throughout the process. Quality is inbred into the process rather than checked outside of the process. The first thing a production employee does when pulling a part or product is to validate, a Total Quality Check, the previous work content. People, even the best employees, can and will make mistakes a small percent of the time. The operator who does TQC and finds an error passes it back to the operation where the error was created.

One thing that cannot be allowed is "two operational" passes. That is a situation in which one team member makes an error and another team member doing TQC does not identify it. These "team" or two operational passes will not be counted toward linearity attainment goals. Quality teams will identify and ask for quality problems to be eliminated. People must be listened to closely about design flaws that contribute to quality problems.

TQC Operational Method Sheets

Illustrated operational method sheets not only tell and show the operator what work is to be performed, they also show what work is to be verified and the total quality control inspection to be done (reference Figure 10-1). Employees can do verification against work performed at the same operation, but they can never do a total quality control inspection against work performed at the same operation. Any time there are multiple ways to perform work and only one way is correct, later in the process a total quality inspection must be performed at another operation. Total quality does not require employees to verify everything, but rather very specific elements of work. Total quality precisely directs the employee to specific points of verification and total quality validation. These TQC points are also guides to design engineering for "designed-for-defect" points, which should be corrected. Sometimes, TQC points are covered up in the process and cannot be checked later. These products will be identified as Acceptable Quality Level (AQL) products until the design for defect is eliminated and design for TQC producibility

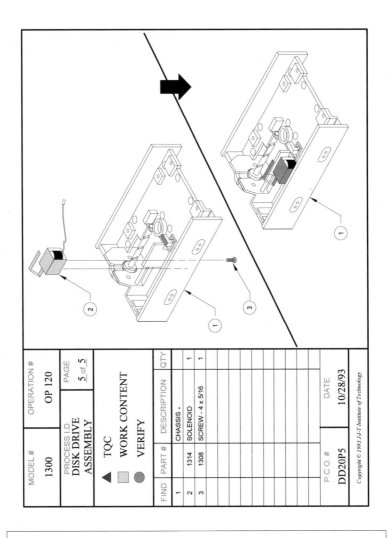

Figure 10-1 TQC Operational Method Sheet

is incorporated. Other points, while verifiable, are not "fail-safe." That is a situation in which there is more than one way to do the work, but each way is correct. Such design dilemmas should be set in priority for elimination through the employee involvement process. New products being released from design will be reviewed on the transfer team methodization process and designed-for-defect points eliminated.

Targeting Process Capability

Quality products are the direct result of a quality process. In *total quality* Demand Flow manufacturing, the quality process is designed before the first product is built. Total quality control at the source seeks to eliminate the opportunity for quality problems and for breakdown to occur. *World-class* manufacturing designs the product for total quality, designs the process to create a quality product, and then takes total quality to the employee. Process capability (Cp) techniques are utilized and defined as the ratio between the design specification width and the observed process capability. It is the design specification width divided by the observed process specification width. The quality process will target the design center, or the nominal value (reference Figure 10-2).

In total quality control, variation to the process must be identified and eliminated. Variations create a broad process specification and result in inconsistency and poor quality performance. Process capabilities must be within the design specification and the target value must be the design center.

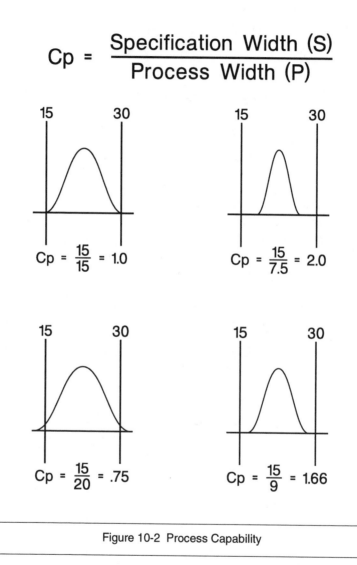

$$Cp = \frac{\text{Specification Width (S)}}{\text{Process Width (P)}}$$

Figure 10-2 Process Capability

As the process capability value increases from 1.00 to 1.66 and on to 2.00, and so on, in-process inventories and scrap will also be reduced.

To ensure adherence to the targeted design center, process capability (Cpk) related to the design center is also measured.

$$Cp = \frac{Specification\ Width\ (S)}{Process\ Width\ (P)}$$

$$Cpk = (\,1 - [\,K\,]\,)\,Cp$$

$$K = \frac{D - (\bar{x})}{S/2}$$

$$D\ =\ Design\ Center$$
$$(\bar{x})\ =\ Process\,Average$$

The total quality Demand Flow process will always target actual performance to be within the process specification of a part or product. This means processes drifting out of process control can be noticed prior to the point where they fall outside of the design specification and create scrap and rework. A production process with a process capability (Cpk) greater than one, but less than the designed Cpk, is producing good products in the eyes of the customer via the design specification but is a warning sign that the process may be drifting out of control. The objective through the TQC process perfection program is to tighten the observed process capability while the design specification remains constant. This will cause the Cpk ratio to rise. In the TQC Demand Flow process, if the process capability is less than one, the dual-card Kanban technique and in-process inspection should be employed. When Cpk is less than one, this dictates that the process cannot consistently meet the design specifications. The dual-card Kanban technique enables production to be started in a quantity that is greater than the consuming process's pull quantity. The additional produce quantity is necessary because of yield and/or process problems. Until the problems can be solved, a temporary retreat is made—larger quantities of units are produced each time. On machines with a Cpk of less than one, scrap or rework will occur, and more units must be produced at a time to make up for the yield problem.

Experimentation of Design Techniques

Design experiments is a tool which is essential in identifying and eliminating dangerous process variation for the purpose of establishing and maintaining control over any given process. Characteristic of a process that is in statistical control is that it will be repeatable, stable and predictable. The total quality manufacturer is primarily after prevention techniques. The data gathered will be simple, visible, and specific to the operations and the machines. *Quality products are the direct result of a quality process.* Focus should be placed on fixing the process rather than the more costly alternative of inspecting and fixing the product. Quality should be bred into the design of a product and into the process via methods rather than through external inspection. Every defect has a cause, every cause a solution. The solution is found through the TQC/employee involvement process.

Process Perfection Program

An operational pareto is maintained at every operation in the process to track opportunities for improvement and the number of occurrences of each opportunity. This information is maintained by the production employees in quality notebooks. Each employee, each team, each support organization, and the division as a whole will have prominently posted paretos identifying opportunities for improvement (reference Figure 10-3). Dangerous "designed-for-defect" flaws and other known problems can be predefined on the pareto so that the employee can easily track occurrences. The highest priority on the pareto will be identified from the left, typically the problem/opportunity with the greatest number of occurrences. The trend of meeting product specifications within the process specification is also maintained. Teams identify occurrences of problems/opportunities and assign them to the related areas or support teams and the people on those support teams.

Problems Are Opportunities

The problems are treated like opportunities, and this information is posted prominently. Root causes are identified, responsibility assigned and data gathered. Control charts will be utilized to ensure process capability. Problems will be noted prior to the process getting out of design specification. The process may be drifting out of control well before a "bad" part or product is produced. Process control charts will identify problems/opportunities so that corrective action can be taken.

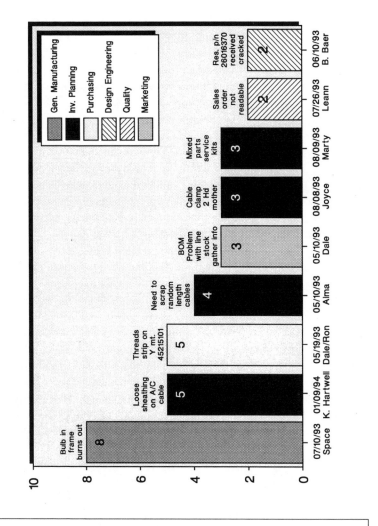

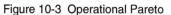

Figure 10-3 Operational Pareto

Experimentation of design techniques will also be used for supplier tracking on problem parts. Often manufacturers discover that they have attempted to drive a particular part well beyond its capability or beyond the capability of the product/process. The operational pareto will be the format for collecting data to identify the problem and point the way to the solution. A "fishboning" technique will be used to identify all possible causes of a problem and isolate the probable cause via cause-and-effect analysis (reference Figure 10-4).

Continual Improvement Goal

Everyone on the process perfection or employee involve-ment team must be trained to brainstorm and maintain a pareto chart, control chart and understand fishbone analyses. The focus of the TQC Demand Flow manufacturer is to take quality to the employee/machine level. For every problem, there is an oppor-tunity. For every opportunity, there is a plan. Problem solving is tracked: who has had the problem; how long have they had it; what are they doing about it? The entire process is kept highly visible. Causes in the process are eliminated by permanent solutions, fixing the manufacturing process, redesign and employee training. The process is continuously monitored. If the targeted problem goes away, the true cause has been found, the problem is solved, and it is time to move on to the next opportunity. The goal is to continually improve the process. The standard is perfection against process capability at the point of value.

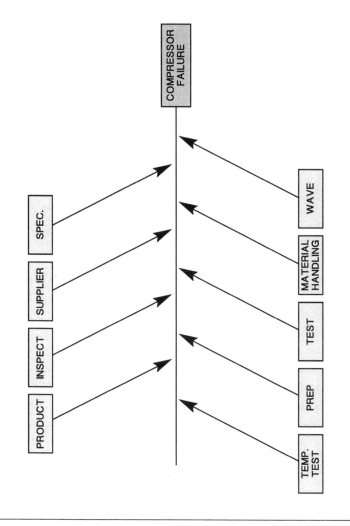

Figure 10-4 Fishbone

Excellence Is Focus of All Personnel

The focus is on process perfection and problem solving. The force employed includes the total participation of all people in the company. Problem solving at the *world-class* company is everyone's responsibility, from the entry-level employee to the chief executive officer. Everyone is associated with a TQC team. **Employee involvement is the most powerful aspect of the program.** The resulting improved quality means customer satisfaction, improved productivity and improved profit.

Chapter Eleven

Demand Flow
Financial Management

C hanging the financial and management reporting systems to be consistent with the responsive Demand Flow Business Strategy becomes a prerequisite for leading the change away from a departmental financial costing system. With flexible processes and production employees, direct labor is no longer tracked nor is it the basis for the application of overhead costs. The clear focus is on material and overhead costs, **not** direct labor. It would be very confusing to implement Demand Flow manufacturing without changing the financial system. Labor-based costing techniques can create a negative illusion as the highly productive flow process shrinks the labor basis.

Financial control and management in a Demand Flow manufacturing environment are very important and significantly different from traditional manufacturing techniques. Traditionally, the old three-bucket approach is used:

- Raw material in the storeroom (RAW)

- Work-In-Process (WIP)

- Finished Goods Inventory (FGI)

In schedulized manufacturing, individual work orders are scheduled and material is issued to build a specific quantity of a specific assembly or fabricated part. Each unique work order is carefully tracked in detail to collect the issued material, production labor and the corresponding overhead. There is no reporting of WIP variances until the production work order closes. Physical inventories have proven that the actual work-in-process inventory seldom matches the book work-in-process inventory. Traditionally, it takes weeks or months to complete production assigned to a work order and for the product to go through the process and to report the corresponding results.

Accuracy, Availability, Adaptability

The primary objective of Demand Flow manufacturing finance is to provide management with information— information that is accurate and timely. Financial organizations must be adaptable enough to produce information which is based upon the needs of DFT management. In addition to being accurate and timely, the data must be obtained at a reasonable cost. The DFT manufacturer must look at the product as a flow process. Little data should be collected until a product is completed and backflushed. The product is built in the flow process—the data is collected at the end of the process. Data sought in the financial accounting system is:

- Cost of the product—to be able to price the product properly

- Value of the inventory on hand—to satisfy the reporting needs internally and externally

- Controlling costs—to monitor the cost of the production and operating activities

- Simulation—the ability to adjust product volume and mix to evaluate various margin scenarios

The only data that must be collected while a product is in the process is scrap. Scrap data must be collected whenever and wherever scrap occurs. Otherwise, the bill of material data is used exclusively to account for the material to be purchased and eventually consumed in the product. This planned consumption occurs when the product leaves production and its parts are backflushed—relieved from raw-in-process inventory.

Monitoring Product Costs

Product cost accounting in the Demand Flow manufacturing environment includes the planned material consumption from the flat bill of material measured at the final backflush point only. Material overhead (acquisition cost) is applied as a percentage against the product's Raw Material at its Standard

Material cost, and any extra usage and scrap transactions are recorded by exception. Companywide homogeneous overhead is applied against the total product cycle time. Under the Demand Flow Business Strategy, Flow-Based™ Costing techniques are utilized to establish a standard product cost by taking material content of each product and adding the accumulated operational costs (overhead). Actual product cost per unit is calculated by totaling operational costs for the process during a given period of time and dividing that amount by the number of units produced during that time period. This calculation would yield actual operational cost per unit.

Labor De-emphasized

The Demand Flow companies have demonstrated an uncanny ability to focus on material cost—a far greater ability than that of most schedulized companies. Emphasis in the United States for many years has been on labor costs, even though labor on most efficient processes has dropped to between five and 15 percent of product cost. Meanwhile, the material and overhead portion of total product cost has soared to 85 to 95 percent.

The classic example of this outdated focus is the struggling American automobile company that refused to shut down its line, even though lack of demand suggested that rationale: for years management pressured that an idle line would cost the company $850 per minute. Unfortunately, they kept their lines running to produce excessive inventories and eventually sold these products at a loss. Under the Demand Flow Business

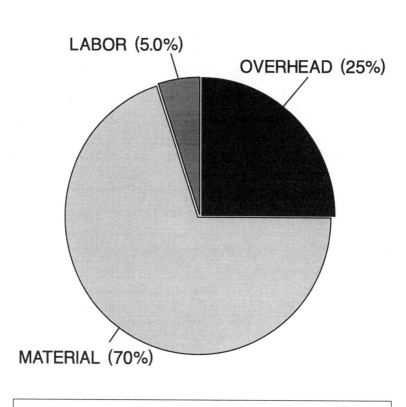

Figure 11-1 Product Cost Percentages

Strategy, the line volume should have been slowed or adjusted to match market demand. Under Demand Flow manufacturing the focus is on the lion's share of product cost: material and overhead. The basic premise in DFT cost accounting is that the direct labor portion of the product cost is shrinking and is too small to warrant detailed tracking. The total product cycle time is short enough that the labor portion of inventory value moves through the product process quickly. The amount of inventory in the Demand Flow process is relatively small.

Flow-Based Overheads

Demand Flow manufacturing applies homogeneous overhead to total product cycle time for several reasons. Applying homogeneous overhead to total product cycle time does not penalize production for becoming more efficient. Total product cycle time has a direct relationship with the amount of homogeneous overhead consumed and the rate at which inventory turns over. Traditionally, applying overhead to direct labor increases the amount of overhead per production head count if production becomes more efficient and labor work at an operation is eliminated. Applying overhead to material will dangerously increase the amount of overhead applied if an assembly or fabricated part is subcontracted out and the standard material cost is increased, or if two products with similar work content are made from materials of vastly different value. Applying overhead to material will create a focus on reducing material costs and turn into a supplier cost reduction program. This also removes the focus from the production process which in turn sacrifices the benefits achieved through the continuous improvement of the TQC flow process.

Establishing the Standard Product Cost

The standard product cost will still contain the basic elements associated with:

- Material

- Labor

- Overhead

Labor (direct and indirect) will **not** be tracked against an operational efficiency standard. Since production employees are now required to move to fill "holes" created in processes that are producing at less than capacity, exactly *which* person produced *what* quantity is considered to be inaccurate and meaningless information. Labor costs will become an element of overhead costs.

Overhead costs now contain common labor costs, and this homogeneous overhead cost will be applied to the total product cycle time for each product. Other variable overhead costs can also be charged per square foot of manufacturing space occupied, per hour of planned usage, and product-specific resource requirements.

The total annual overhead cost is determined as the sum of the common labor costs, at an average hourly wage (labor/hour), plus the fixed overhead costs per year. The sum of these costs to convert purchased material into a finished product will include: fixed costs, variable costs and labor costs which form a homogeneous overhead pool. This homogeneous overhead pool will contain conversion costs that are applicable to all products. Also, a variable overhead cost may be created to account for extraordinary conversion costs driven by the use of special machines or resources. These extraordinary overhead costs would be absorbed by only the products that require the use of these costly resources. This extraordinary overhead cost could also be allocated based on the square footage that the manufacturing process occupies.

$$Homogeneous\ Overhead\ (\$AOH) = (P \times \$AVG) + \$OH$$

where:

P = Planned Annual Production Employee Hours (The sum of Planned annual volume x SOE labor times)

$AVG = Average Production Wage per Hour

$OH = Overhead Costs per Year (Fixed and variable, but not extraordinary conversion costs)

The basis for the application of the *Homogeneous Overhead* will be the Total Product Cycle Time of each product. In order to achieve this, a cost of *Homogeneous Overhead per TP c/t hour ($TP c/t Hour)* must be established.

$$\$TP\ c/t\ Hour = \frac{\$AOH}{Annual\ Planned\ TP\ c/t\ Hours}$$

where:

$AOH =$ Annual Homogeneous Overhead

Annual Planned TP c/t Hours =
>Annual planned volume of each product times its TP c/t, in hours.

Example:

*Annual Homogeneous Overhead = $12,000,000
(includes fixed
costs and
labor costs)*

	Planned Volume	Total Product Cycle Time	Annual Planned TP c/t Hours
Product "A"	1250 units	6.8 hours	8500 hours
Product "B"	568 units	6.8 hours	3862 hours
Product "C"	1100 units	3.0 hours	3300 hours

Annual Planned TP c/t Hours = 15,662 hours

To calculate $TP c/t Hour:

Homogeneous Overhead per TP c/t Hour = $\dfrac{\$12,000,000}{15,662}$
($TP c/t Hour)

$TP c/t Hour = $766 per TP c/t Hour

Applying *Homogeneous Overhead per TP c/t Hour* on each product's Total Product Cycle Time may not account for all costs to produce the product or product family. Two products could have the same TP c/t, but one of the products may require an expensive machine while the other does not. It may be more equitable to apply the cost of the expensive machine only on the product that requires this resource. If this is the case, the extraordinary cost of conversion should be applied to that specific product or family of products.

Example:

Product "A" requires the use of a $500,000 machine.

Product "B" does not require this machine.

Product "C" does not require this machine.

The cost of this machine should be applied to only Product "A."

To allocate this extraordinary overhead cost, square footage of the process could be used as a basis and only Product "A" would bear the cost. Based upon this extraordinary overhead cost, a cost per 1000 square feet of manufacturing occupancy, applicable only to Product "A" can now be computed.

The application of the extraordinary overhead costs such as depreciation, specific machine maintenance and utilities is accomplished by structuring specific accounts/subaccounts into a cost pool that is driven by machine hours to the specific activity that consumes the specific machine process.

Caution: There is a tendency to over manage extraordinary overhead costs. Do not microscopically explore your facility for these costs. They should be obvious and readily apparent.

Purchased Material Content

To establish the Total Product Cost, the purchased material content of a product must also be identified. The bill of material in Demand Flow Technology must be 100 percent accurate in order to backflush inventory. Each product's bill of material will be costed out at a Total Raw Material Standard Cost. Purchase Price Variance will be measured by comparing the actual purchased price versus the Raw Material Standard Cost. The Cost of Carrying inventory should also be added to the Total Cost of the Raw Material, not to the standard raw material cost.

$$\frac{RM\ standard\ cost + Acquisition\ cost}{Total\ RM\ standard\ cost}$$

To establish Product Cost in Demand Flow cost accounting, the following factors would be used:

$$\frac{\$TP\ c/t\ Hour\ x\ TP\ c/t + extraordinary\ variable\ OVERHEAD\ costs + Total\ RM\ standard\ cost}{Product\ cost}$$

Standard Cost Example:
MODEL - 494X
(Product "A")

Total Product Cycle Time   = 6.8 Hours

Total RM Standard Cost = $8,371.50
Homogeneous Overhead per TP c/t Hour = $766
Extraordinary Variable Overhead Costs = $65 per unit (allocation of cost of specific expensive machine)

PRODUCT STANDARD COST

$ 5,208.80   [$766 x 6.8 *TP c/t Hours*]
+ $ 65.00
+ $ 8,371.50
$13,645.30

In the analysis of actual costs versus planned standard costs, the actual overhead and actual TP c/t would be used. Physical audits of TP c/t to monitor progress and to prove the computerized calculation of TP c/t are quite common responsibilities of the DFT financial organizations.

In actual product cost analysis, actual material scrap costs, if any, would be added to the actual bill of material costs. Although very difficult to accomplish, an actual overhead variance is expected and achieved by reducing the total product cycle time. This variance must be part of the management objective, and this reduction should be targeted and budgeted.

Valuing In-Process Inventory

In trying to obtain the value of RIP (Raw and In-Process), we consider that in a high inventory turn Demand Flow process, the added dollar value of in-process may be insignificant when the inventory is contained within a single flow process that does not have staging points. The flow out of raw and in-process must be and is measured at the end of the process. Quantities in the process can be determined by knowing the process capacity and whether the process is full or empty.

In calculating overhead value in RIP inventory, we consider that at some early stage of the flow process, the product that is being produced is ten percent complete, in the middle of the flow process it is 50 percent complete, and toward the end of the flow process, 90 percent complete. In a Takt time-designed Demand Flow line, the average overhead cost per unit in-process is calculated by dividing the standard overhead cost per unit by two. This homogeneous principle considers that each unit in-process is, on an average, 50 percent complete. The overhead value in RIP is determined by multiplying the sum of the number of operations plus the in-process Kanban quantity times the standard overhead cost divided by two. For an example refer to Figure 11-2, Overhead Value in RIP. The number of in-process Kanbans is 12, and there are also 12 different operations. The overhead cost per unit is $766, and the line is a balanced Demand Flow process. The calculations would be as follows:

$$\frac{766}{2} \; x \; 12 = \$4,596$$

The value of RIP is:

$$
\begin{aligned}
Material\ Value &= \$1,260,000 \\
Overhead\ Value &= \$\quad\ \ 4,596 \\
Total\ RIP\ Value &= \$1,264,596
\end{aligned}
$$

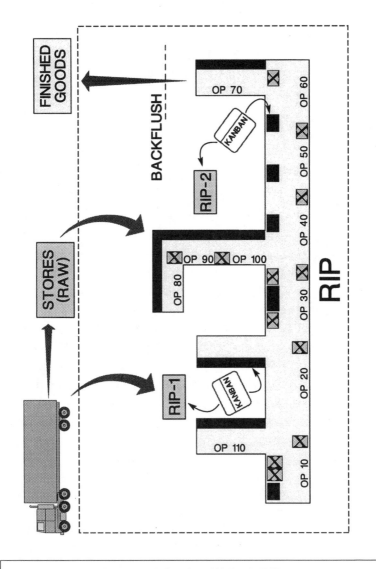

Figure 11-2 Overhead Value in RIP

Changing Departmental to Flow-Based Costing

In changing from departmental and schedulized manufacturing with labor-based cost accounting to flow-based costing techniques, the production process must be changed first. Once changed to the DFT, the financial organization must be able to audit and calculate costs within the flow process. The new role of accounting is to change from labor and work order tracking in multiple departments to flow-based process accounting. Financial managers will become more influential in a decision-making and analytical function as opposed to the traditional roll of tracking transactions. Once the DFT company has adapted the Demand Flow Business Strategy, the emphasis will focus on customer response (no late shipments), zero working capital, inventory turns and the elimination of the unnecessary overhead. Financial managers **must** understand Demand Flow Business Strategy as they will be expected to help lead the pursuit of the *"elite"* zero working capital company.

Chapter Twelve

Achieving a Commitment for World-Class Excellence

The adoption of Demand Flow manufacturing technology should not be an optional choice for the various organizations or individuals in a company committed to becoming a *world-class* manufacturer. It is a technology that, once adopted, must be fully supported by top management and driven across all organizational boundaries. It is a companywide program in which management must be aware of people who are resisting the change—the drive to *world-class* Demand Flow Technology adoption is a cautious one. The Demand Flow manufacturing methodology is focused on the two major elements of product costs: material and overhead. Demand Flow manufacturing techniques are used to develop a powerful production process that utilizes pull systems with in-process quality as the number one objective. Achieving the elite goal of *world-class* manufacturing requires the establishment of nontraditional goals and the implementation of nontraditional methods of managing the process.

Several different tools can be utilized to manage the Demand Flow process. Such tools include TP c/t, flow rate, linearity index measurement, team passes for nonquality items, the number of line stops or time per problem, in-process Kanbans, inventory turns, and employee involvement.

Top management must be committed and supportive to the Demand Flow manufacturing technology. The path is difficult and mined by traditional "we're unique" and "it can't work here" mindsets, but the tremendous benefits are key to the significant growth and financial objectives of the corporation. Top management must stay committed and supportive and express two clear messages:

1. As an employee who is important to the success of the company:

YOU HAVE A VOICE

2. There is no question of our commitment, since:

WE DON'T HAVE A CHOICE

Measuring a TQC Demand Flow Line

The most important goal of a *world-class* production process is to produce a total quality product. Quality is never compromised for any reason. Once the quality of a product is assured, the next goal is to make quality products equal to the daily rate. If the daily rate is 100 units for today, the goal will be to make 100 units—not 95, not 105, but the 100-unit daily rate. The method of measuring and auditing a Demand Flow process is significantly different from measurements in traditional manufacturing. With the flexible employee, individual performance measurement is not possible. All measures will be team measures.

Cycle Time Monitored

The Demand Flow manufacturer should monitor the total product cycle time of the flow process. If the calculated total product cycle time is one hour, the manufacturer should physically go to the production process and audit this time. Unfortunately, it is not possible to audit actual total product cycle time by remote control—it must be physical. If process improvements have been made since the last audit, it may be reasonable to expect the total product cycle time to be reduced. We would then underabsorb overhead for that process.

Also closely monitored will be the linearity index. Once a 96 to 98 percent linearity index against the daily rate is achieved, the Demand Flow manufacturer may start to measure actual production flow rates at the back of the process. An 80 to 85 percent linearity index against flow rates is an excellent flow line—on the brink of *world-class* performance.

Support team resources should be close to the process they support. It is the responsibility of the team leader to get these resources when process problems occur. Support team resources cannot be remote control either—they must be in a position to respond quickly to process problems.

Team Pass

A team, or two operational, pass is another measurement of a total quality flow line performance. This occurs if the unit was produced incorrectly and not correctly validated at the following TQC operation. The unit will be returned for rework. Although the reworked unit is now perfectly acceptable from a customer, marketing and financial perspective, it will not be counted toward the daily production linearity goal. The use of a team pass can invoke powerful peer pressure in the process. If a unit requires rework, it is tagged with the pass of the team responsible for the rework. The unit goes through the entire balance of the process with the team pass. The product is not credited to the team goal. There is no way to make up for the team pass, and there is no way to regain credit for the reworked unit. Just like defective work in a customer's hands, non-TQC work in the plant represents a nonrecoverable situation. The percent of team passes and deviations against the daily rate is tracked each day. Reference Figure 12-1 for linearity results of a two operational team pass.

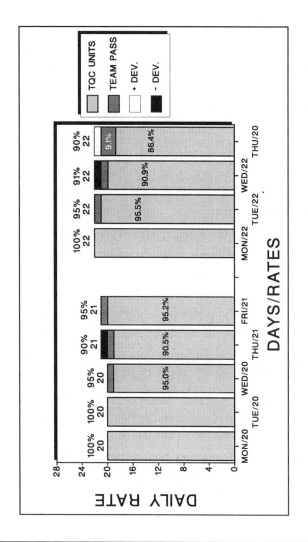

Figure 12-1 Linearity of a Two Operational Team Pass

Management Lights

Switches on the line, accessible to all employees, provide management with an accurate and continuous monitor of how the Demand Flow line is running. Each Demand Flow line has one set of management lights to communicate the overall status of the entire line. This management light system has a green, red and yellow light. Each production employee has immediate access to a red and yellow switch. If no switches are activated on the line, the management light system will indicate a green condition. Green exists automatically in the absence of another status condition. If there is a need to replenish a raw material Kanban, the employees will activate a switch that flashes a yellow light at the workstation as well as on the management lights. This indicates to the material handlers roving the process that there is material in need of replenishment at the point of the yellow light. They must go to that location, read the Kanban identifying the part and the point of supply, and get material back to the line within a predetermined replenishment time.

If operators in the line cannot work in their primary position or one-up, one-down for some reason, such as machine break-down or a lost tool, the status switch is activated to indicate a red-light state. The red light does not indicate that the entire process has stopped, only that there is a problem at a particular operation in the process that can eventually shut down the process. There is only one management red light in the process. The ideal sequence—minimal delays, adequate people and material—would be yellow with intermittent green flashes and occasional reds.

Timely Replenishment

It is perfectly acceptable in a Demand Flow process for employees to replenish their own material. RIP areas, by definition, are proximate to the process. If production employees are out of material, they will move in the direction of the pull, which in this case is to the appropriate RIP to replenish material. This is done on an exception basis— employees will replenish their own material only when the material handler cannot replenish the Kanban quantity in the allotted time. If employees are expected to replenish their own material on a regular basis, this activity should be included in the TQC sequence of events for that process.

Management's Accordion

The Demand Flow production process can produce between 100 percent and 50 percent of the designed volume with as much ease as the opening and closing of an accordion. Half of the employees can be pulled out of a line—every other employee— and the line will function as smoothly, only at about half the rate. Voids can be filled or created on the Demand Flow line to vary the daily rate with the aid of the flexible employees.

Reporting in a Demand Flow Process

Individual employee tracking and reporting in a Demand Flow process is neither feasible nor desirable with the flexible employee. The reporting in a Demand Flow process will be simple, direct and meaningful. Labor and machine content per product/process in total hours per unit will be known and reported. This will be the basis for how many people will be needed in the process at a given rate. Cycle time, both total product and operational, will be monitored. Two operational or team passes will be monitored and reported. The number and duration of line stops will be tracked. Inventory levels of purchased material and in-process Kanbans will be monitored and reported. Continual improvement in these measures will be expected through the employee involvement program. Paretos, control charts and fishbones will be utilized extensively. Reporting will be very visible and on a team basis. Managing a production process also involves maintaining employee certification charts and criteria and determining where each employee's primary position will be on a daily basis.

Chapter Thirteen

Computer Role in Competitive Manufacturing

The technology and methodology of Demand Flow manufacturing drastically change the role of the formal computer system. Many of the execution techniques of Demand Flow manufacturing can be done without a computer. The computer must become a tool to support Demand Flow Technology manufacturing. A computer can make it easier to do such things as:

- Calculate operational cycle time

- Calculate total product cycle time

- Establish a Demand-Based daily rate production plan

- Manage the Kanban tools

- Demand-Based Forecasting of material and resource feasibility planning

- Calculate the application of overhead to TP c/t

- Process efficiency for management reporting

- Production linearity for management reporting

- Actual versus planned production employee efficiency

- Method sheet management

- Supplier management

Some of these tasks can be done without any computer system; the formal Demand Flow manufacturing computer system must assist in these nontraditional tasks or it becomes of little value in the future. Thus, in a conversion from traditional manufacturing to flow manufacturing, there exists a potentially powerful ally in the computer. The techniques and role of the computer—the way most companies use it in traditional schedulized manufacturing (MRP II) and the way they would use it in Demand Flow manufacturing—will change drastically. In Demand Flow manufacturing, computer operations are far more simple; the number of computer transactions is substantially lower. The reliance on the computer is much less in Demand Flow manufacturing from a transactional standpoint and from the type of computer needed. However, it may be easier to do Demand Flow manufacturing without a computer than MRP II with a computer (reference Figure 13-1).

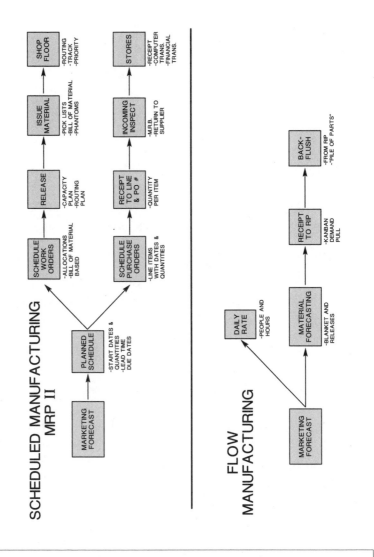

Figure 13-1 Computer Role in Flow Manufacturing

Typically, most traditional companies find the conversion to Demand Flow manufacturing difficult without a computer. Unfortunately, some narrow-minded individuals attempt to crutch their current traditional computer systems with independent spreadsheet and database tools. This typically leads to a dangerous misinformation problem with bad management and financial reporting! Toyota and many other major flow manufacturing Japanese companies do not use computers for the planning and execution of their flow manufacturing processes. However, the computer can assist in the line design, daily management and planning, and in the forecasting and control of material to and from suppliers. Historically, there has been a tremendous difference between the focus of Japanese flow manufacturing techniques and the American MRP II tools designed for the computer. Americans attempting to do traditional manufacturing are still much more reliant on computers than is the corresponding Japanese manufacturer.

Personal Computer Power

When converting from MRP II to Demand Flow Technology, the type of computer needed may shift from powerful, centralized mainframes to individual workstations of personal computers attached via a Local Area Network (LAN) for two main reasons: first, the personal computer is becoming very powerful; and second, there are far fewer transactions in Demand Flow manufacturing. Thus, we are continually seeing $60 million, $80 million and even $100 million businesses that can now feasibly run their Demand Flow manufacturing systems on personal computer Local Area Networks that may also be tied to corporate computer networks. The personal computer in recent years has put the specialized computing power into the hands of the user. Previously, such power was highly centralized, highly bureaucratic, and guarded from a technological standpoint. Now, the more powerful personal computer gets the actual information closer to the user and on a timely basis—when and where it is most needed. The traditional information systems department no longer have total control over the applications. Users are no longer bound by the development and enhancements from very large traditional software suppliers. The Demand Flow manufacturing computer software and system must be as flexible and responsive as the manufacturing technology it serves.

Traditional System Evolution

Material planning initially meant exploding a bill of material simply to calculate the purchased material needed for a product. As the traditional computer system evolved into MRP I (Material Requirement Planning), along with the use of a multilevel subassembly bill of material, additional sophistication was added. In addition to directing what to buy, MRP I also showed what to make and when to schedule its start. MRP II brought additional enhancements in scheduling and continued the evolution of a sophisticated routing and tracking system. It tracked each assembly or fabricated part and the corresponding materials, labor and overhead throughout the process. It became a scheduling tool, a management tool, a batch producing Economic Order Quantity (EOQ) production tool, and an operator efficiency measurement tool. Work orders for multilevel assemblies or fabricated parts were tracked through independent departments and work centers, tracking the corresponding material and labor. The system also kept track of purchase orders and the related delivery dates and quantities. And it kept track of each work order on the shop floor. It would tell planners what to schedule and storeroom employees what parts to issue. The system completely tracked where material was, both in the storeroom and in the work-in-process. MRP II evolved into labor-based accounting and planning systems that were very sophisticated and enabled the tracking of multilevel products through multilevel departments while offering some promise of controlling the traditionally complicated manufacturing process.

Ruled the Roost

MRP II systems became very big, very bulky and very unmanageable. They tended to proliferate management reports. In effect, the MRP II system is management by report. The difficult task becomes: which report to use and how to use it most effectively.

- MRP: bill of material exploded to indicate what to buy and when to buy it.

- MRP I: what to build, when it must be scheduled, what to buy, when it must be bought.

- MRP II: the push philosophy includes a sophisticated system of order tracking, order launching, expediting, queue reporting, multilevel bills of material, job costing, dispatch lists, shop floor control, expedite lists, capacity requirements planning, kit issues, work order receipts, queues and lead time, work order scheduling, labor-based accounting and management by report.

Formal Path to Demand Flow Manufacturing

In the Demand Flow manufacturing pull philosophy, the computer becomes a valuable tool when used for:

- Backflush transactions to get material out of the process

- Engineering operational evaluations

- Operational line balancing

- Daily process linearity calculations

- Linear rate indexing

- Kanban management

- Kanban pull sequencing

- Kanban sizing

- Calculating operational cycle times

- Calculating total product cycle times

- Financial applications of overhead to TP c/t

- Method sheet design and management

- TQC sequence of events

- Develop Demand-Based rate planning (rather than scheduling)

- Process accounting standards from the sequence of events

Demand Flow Technology emphasizes management by eyes and management through use of people rather than attempting to manage externally by reports. Demand Flow manufacturing techniques substantially reduce the number of reports, part numbers and, eventually, suppliers. Blanket purchase contracts are used in Demand Flow manufacturing and releases are made against these contracts. The computer in Demand Flow manufacturing is also used to track contracts, transportation networks and packaging considerations from the purchasing standpoint rather than in the traditional use of detailed scheduled purchase orders. Typically, company computer transactions will be reduced between 50 percent and 90 percent in flow manufacturing as compared with MRP II. In Demand Flow manufacturing the computer is not used for scheduling, picking kits, routing or tracking. Immediately, this tends to render the MRP II shop floor control system useless. The formal Demand Flow manufacturing system becomes a simpler and more concise management tool. The time and complexity of use of computers in manufacturing peaked with MRP II and has decreased with Demand Flow manufacturing.

Computer Modifications

In making the conversion from schedulized subassembly manufacturing to Demand Flow manufacturing, the computer can be a powerful aid in the transition. Significant modifications in the computer system and/or acquisition of additional Demand Flow manufacturing software is usually necessary to make the conversion and to enable the existing system to meet the simplified demands of the Demand Flow methodology.

Traditionally, there is a standard routing, and this has *no* relationship to the TQC sequence of events. The traditional MRP II routing system relies upon the bill of material to structure independent processes, fabricated parts, and subassemblies. In Demand Flow manufacturing, the bill of material is a "pile of parts," and the process is controlled through the TQC sequence of events. The TQC sequence of events requires support on the computer to identify what events of the sequence of events are value-added and nonvalue-added, which steps are setup, which are move, and most important, to identify the quality criteria for each element of work. Once the information has been entered into the computer, it can help identify the targeted work content and quality criteria for each operation. This is based upon the targeted operational cycle time calculation established during line design. This is a very valuable tool during the initial flow line design as well as for the ongoing process improvement design changes. The computer can also assist in the identification of any nonvalue-added events in the TQC sequence of events. It becomes a valuable management tool in determining what should be attacked for reducing the total product cycle time.

The bill of material system in Demand Flow manufacturing must include the backflush location information and, in many cases, intermediate deduct identification information. The Demand Flow manufacturing bill of material computer system should also include a "pending file" in the engineering change system. The "pending file" is essential in maintaining the correct backflush effectivity dates. It authorizes the procurement of new materials based upon the approved date of an engineering change, but it does not change the actual bill of material in the process until the part(s) are obtained and consumed into the product.

True computer systems to support the Demand Flow Technology are in their early maturity stages, and their development is moving rapidly as more and more forward-looking companies abandon the MRP II methodology and adopt the Demand Flow methodology. Of course, most MRP II software packages now claim to support the flow philosophy. Unfortunately, the only thing changed is the brochure listing Just-In-Time and the scheduling page recommending the reduction of the "lot size to 1."

Flexible Demand Based Planning System

The Demand Flow manufacturing rate-based planning system must be able to accommodate functions that the typical MRP II scheduling systems do not perform. This includes such things as flex fence management tools, forecast consumption tools to blend forecasts and actual orders, the ability to plan and view resource requirements without using work orders, daily flow rates and resource calculations to see how many people it takes to support a particular daily rate, total product cycle time calculations to recommend demand and planning time fences, daily forecast violation reporting, actual flow rate performance, and linearity reporting in the production process. The daily rates are established at the back of the process as opposed to the scheduling techniques and systems that attempt to control the front of the process.

Formal "Pile of Parts" and Engineering Tools

The bill of material is important in traditional manufacturing, but it is doubly critical in Demand Flow manufacturing. It not only controls the parts to buy, but it also controls the inventory. The bill of material requirements of a Demand Flow system should have the capability of taking a traditional multi-level bill of material and compressing it into a single-level bill of material. If you are designing a Demand Flow system, you should give the user the capability of determining whether the subassembly part number should be eliminated, should be restructured independently as a FRU, or should remain as an additional level on the bill of material. Other major changes in the creation of a bill of material's format include the Demand Flow manufacturing "pending file." This allows the material requirements planning algorithm to correctly identify and plan the purchase of parts associated with the engineering change order based upon the approval date of the engineering change order, but will not yet modify the bill of material for backflush or configuration control purposes. The bill of material system must also contain backflush locations and deduct identification information. Although there is only one bill of material, different lines (line IDs) in different plants can have different backflush locations and deduct identification information. The bill of material "where-used" system must have the capability to identify which method sheet contains a specific part number. If an engineering change affects a specific part number, the design and process engineer needs to know what method sheets are affected when the change is approved.

Backflush and Kanban Inventory Control

The bill of material must also have the capability of identifying the backflush information required for inventory management and control. Intermediate backflush capability at a user-defined deduct point should also be provided. The single-level bill of material is a key to a lower number of transactions. In traditional manufacturing, material requirements planning individually processes through each level of the bill of material, whether or not there are any requirements for each level of the bill of material. Computer processing goes through those levels one by one. This is one reason why material requirements planning runs in large companies may take an entire weekend to complete and process. Because of the Demand Flow manufacturing flat bill of material, along with the elimination of the work order system logic, material requirements planning can now run in a fraction of the time.

TQC Method Sheet Coordination

Method sheet information should also be kept on the bill of material, and the method identification number should be tied to a line item on the bill of material. As discussed earlier, when an engineering change is made to the flow manufacturing bill of material, the software system can point out the method sheets that are affected and those that may need review and modification. An eventual goal is to link the manufacturing system bill of material with the CAD design systems. With that connection to the design process, CAD information can be used directly by the manufacturing system to aid in method sheet design and bill of material creation. Although the bill of material information may be managed by separate organizations, there should be only one bill of material. The pile of parts will be controlled by the design or product engineering group, whichever is responsible for the form, fit and function of the product. The backflush location and deduct identification information will be controlled by the people in planning or production. The security for the change capability of the bill of material must be segregated accordingly.

Critical Engineering Information

The bill of material system is where all of the critical engineering change and revision information will be kept. If a revision level change is made to a part number, the old revision level, new revision and the nature of the change with the engineering change number should be retained by date. If an engineering change requires a part number change, the ECO "pending file" will be used until the change is actually incorporated into the product. There would be *current* and *pending* engineering change information. The pending bill of material, based on its approval, will be used for the procurement of material, while the current bill of material will be used to build and backflush material out of RIP. Once the change is physically implemented, the status of the changed bill of material will be moved from pending to current.

Kanban Management

The daily management of a Kanban card system should not be underestimated. The formal Demand Flow manufacturing computer system can become an invaluable tool by identifying Kanbans that are in RIP along with the information related to their pull sequence and quantity. The Demand Flow computer system must provide guidance on when changing a Kanban size should be considered. In addition to managing the current Kanbans, the Demand Flow manufacturing system must facilitate the creation of new Kanbans based upon new products on existing lines. Kanban management must also identify any obsolete Kanbans that are no longer required in the current product lines. Sizing, creation and printing of a Kanban card must be based on the replenishment parameters. Companies trying to maintain, independently, a Kanban information system or a manual Kanban system are heading for long-term disaster. Although the execution is quite simple, the task of Kanban management should not be underestimated, particularly in high-growth or high-technology companies.

Managing Flow and Flexibility

The Demand Flow production system should assist in calculating operational cycle time and total product cycle time for each line or cell. This assistance is vital in the design and management of the Demand Flow process.

The Demand-Based planning system should assist with managing the master planning information and the conversion of this data into a daily rate. Based on the manufacturing calendar, the formal Demand Flow system should track actual linearity against the planned daily rate. For purchasing, in addition to keeping track of the negotiated flexibility contained in the purchase contracts, the formal Demand Flow system is used to guide frequency on parts delivery based upon an algorithm that balances transportation costs against inventory carrying costs. It should monitor DFT contracts and measure supplier performance on both early and late deliveries. Delivery performance, flex window management and quality performance information is vital to the management of the DFT company. The DFT system should also keep track of transportation networks, monitor contract performance and assist in minimizing transportation costs.

Advanced Communications Capabilities

The Demand Flow manufacturing purchasing system will also include advanced communication capabilities, such as Electronic Data Interchange (EDI), to minimize the paperwork and transactions. This requires a degree of trust between supplier and buyer. The EDI network, highly utilized in the retail, textile, automobile and electronics industries, provides the capability of enjoying a nearly-paperless system. The release of a part over the EDI network makes available an advance shipment notice from the supplier that the part is shipping. Initially, the advance shipment notice will probably be matched against the receiver and invoice and still do the traditional three-way match that is prevalent today. Eventually, as the relationship grows stronger in trust, the receiver can be eliminated. Eventually, only the invoice and the advance shipment notice would be matched and used as an acknowledgment of a receipt of the material to kick off the payables process. The ultimate goal is acknowledging receipt of the materials at the point of backflush. That optimum result should be achievable for at least a few parts in the process. The ultimate system will not have a requirement for the traditional three-way match before a check can be generated. In the Electronic Data Interchange network, even the check that is paid to the supplier can be automated with payment via electronic funds transfer.

Process Accounting

The cost accounting system will be set up for process accounting: applying overhead to a process and using total product cycle time as the key under which to apply the overhead. Demand Flow manufacturing requires changing from labor-based to process-based accounting systems. Labor now becomes an element of overhead. There will be only two costing elements in the Demand Flow process: material and overhead. Overhead will include a fixed percentage which will be applied across all lines in the plant, and a variable overhead rate which will be applied at specific operations or cells within each line. The computer system will be able to track process variance with the keys being total product cycle time goal versus actual and product costing variance based upon the standard overhead and material credited versus the actual overhead required and actual material consumed.

Inventory Balances Are Backflushed

The formal inventory control system will keep track of the inventory balance in RIP as well as the inventory balances in the storerooms. The inventory control system in the storeroom will probably keep the same location tracking system that is used in traditional manufacturing as long as a storeroom is required. RIP inventory will be categorized independently as a general inventory location. RIP inventory is without relationship to any particular location. The formal system will sum up the inventories in RIP and in the storeroom for a total inventory balance to be used for planning purposes.

Demand Flow Manufacturing Reporting

The DFT manufacturing system should have far fewer reports. Reports will tend to be summary versus detail reports. There will be no 2,000-page purchase orders, overdue reports or expedite reports. What will be reported are such things as linearity by line, product completions, quality analysis data and employee involvement in improvements that are being reported through the plant.

Computers Reflect Processes

The difference is obvious when comparing the processes. The Demand Flow manufacturing pull system uses:

- A Demand-Based system for planning long-range material requirements

- Releases generated against a blanket purchase order for the preferred single supplier

- Material receipts directed to raw-in-process inventory

- Materials relieved by a backflush transaction

Traditional MRP II uses schedules in a push fashion to control the schedule of purchase orders and work orders. After the order is scheduled, material is issued from a storeroom and the work order is released to production. Purchased parts are received from a particular purchase order line item and transacted into the storeroom until they are required to be issued to a work order.

Graphic Orientation

Computer tools and techniques employed in Demand Flow Technology are very graphically oriented. System reporting will use many charts and graphs in reporting data for analysis. Graphic computer techniques are used to create pictorial method sheets, graphics on total quality performance, generation of improvement pareto charts, process capability analysis, fishboning, and so forth. From a manufacturing engineering standpoint, advanced graphics techniques are used to create graphic production documentation rather than the traditional text oriented production documentation.

These graphic production documents or operational method sheets represent an exceptional tool for the quality and performance of work in the process. Verification and total quality control by production employees is now possible. These sheets feature a large colored illustration that graphically directs the operator to points of work and verification. Red lines or other manual modifications will no longer be tolerated as they defeat the TQC thrust of the operational method sheets. Personal computers and technical illustration software can be used to create such sheets in minutes.

Simpler Network Solutions

Software used in a Demand Flow environment can often be PC LAN-based because the number of computer transactions and the amount of memory and disk space that is required will be significantly lower than that of scheduled manufacturing. This is due to several reasons:

- Elimination of several levels of the bill of material

- Elimination of scheduling

- Elimination of kitting

- Elimination of shop floor control tracking

- Elimination of computer transactions between RIP and the line

- The reduction of purchase orders and receiving activities

If personal computers are utilized, the PCs must be networked so all personnel can access needed information. Networks are becoming more common and more powerful. The PC LAN-based manufacturing software must be able to interface with a mainframe. This is necessary in the environments where a company has a corporate order entry or corporate finance system. In those cases, information will need to be uploaded and downloaded between the manufacturing system and the corporate business and financial systems. Since the DFT software can be PC LAN-based and significantly less cumbersome than today's traditional MRP II software, the price of the initial systems and ongoing support can be incredibly lower. Actually, the cost of the PC LAN-based Demand Flow manufacturing software will be significantly lower than the multimillion-dollar investments that companies make today in traditional MRP II systems. And not only will the cost of the DFT computer system be hundreds of thousands of dollars less than the MRP II system, the end result will be better. For example, the FlowPower$^{®}$ Business System from the Jc-I-T Institute of Technology is a comprehensive Demand Flow software system that operates in a client/server environment. The implementation of these PC LAN-based systems, developed on a sound understanding of Demand Flow techniques, will also be much quicker and easier than the lengthy and costly installation of the MRP II systems.

Chapter Fourteen

Implementing the Strategy and Technology

W*orld-class* Demand Flow manufacturing is a company-wide business strategy. Manufacturing can be used as a weapon to compete in today's global economy. It is developed utilizing Demand Flow Technology manufacturing with a focus on speed-to-market and market responsiveness. Demand Flow manufacturing technology reduces new product development time and substantially increases *speed-to-market.* Demand Flow manufacturing seeks to highlight and then eliminate or reduce unnecessary work—defined as anything that is not value-added in the eyes of the customer. Flexible people, employee involvement, operational method sheets, Kanban management style, TQC product development and flow line designs are keys to the market responsiveness in Demand Flow manufacturing. Objectives include a *world-class* level of quality and high inventory turns leading to a higher return on assets. Technology turnover, the rate at which new products are introduced, used to be five to ten years—now it is 18 to 24 months. Demand Flow manufacturing technology is required not only for manufacturing excellence—it is required for the survival of manufacturing into the next century. Demand Flow Technology is a technology that hinges on people, customer satisfaction, Demand Based manufacturing and TQC process technology.

Organization for Implementation

The company-wide project team will be formed as the beginning of the implementation process. A full-time project leader should be named. This individual will report to the top management person in the division, typically the vice president of manufacturing or the plant manager. The team leader should be a person who has solid and general familiarity with the business, is well rounded in the technology and strategy of Demand Flow manufacturing, and who is the type who can get things done despite the inevitable obstacles. The leader must have a good orientation toward people, since people are essential to the successful implementation. An individual who has experience crossing organizational and mindset boundaries is mandatory. The leader **must** be a current employee in the division where implementation is taking place (reference Figure 14-1).

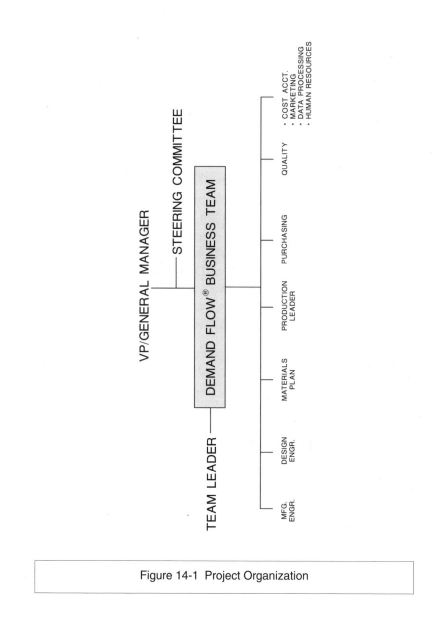

Figure 14-1 Project Organization

Single-Level Management Team

The team leader will form the cornerstone of the implementation steering team. Once selected by the team leader, this steering team will spend a large amount of time on the implementation. Although they will maintain their regular position, they will have the project as a primary responsibility. The team will consist of representatives from design engineering, finance, manufacturing engineering, manufacturing systems, quality, production, planning and materials. They will form the core group for implementation of the specific plant or product line. Support members from human resources, marketing and CAD/document control will be on the team also, but they will act in more of an advisory position. When a major milestone is reached, the core members, with the exception of the team leader, will individually rotate back into their functional positions and new team members will be individually selected. This approach gives specific product/process expertise to the implementation, as well as providing many people with the opportunity of participating actively in the implementation process. The steering team must be hands-on individuals with the authority and the responsibility for implementation. The steering team approves all techniques and methods before the major implementation tasks are even started.

Implementation Starts from the Back

An initial plant and product line should be selected for implementation. The implementation should always begin from the back, or final assembly, portion of a product. Feeder lines and upstream operations can continue to batch and schedule in the meantime, but daily rates of quality units are initially targeted at the end of the process. An area which is important to the business and which will have high visibility should be selected. These implementations must not be allowed to fail—and will not fail—if the focus remains on the Demand Flow Technology. Also, a positive impact on the operation of the business can be felt sooner if a key product/process is selected. Compromises during the early implementation can be extremely dangerous. Early successes must be realized within three to six months of the kickoff. Negative comments by team members, although they will not be tolerated, must be addressed by top management.

Designed with a Consistent Technology

Any new products still in the development stage should be managed and released in a Demand Flow manufacturing mode. This is much easier and more cost effective than taking a product designed in a traditional manner and trying to convert it for Demand Flow manufacturing.

Create an Implementation Plan

The implementation should proceed in an orderly and planned fashion. Steps must be well thought out, taking into consideration all obstacles. Each step must be completed before moving to the next step. Leaving out a key step can lead to negative results and the misguided feeling that Demand Flow manufacturing "can't work here." Implementing a little piece of the Demand Flow Technology here and a little piece there with business-as-usual everywhere else is a true recipe for failure.

Commitment from Top

The implementation process should begin with the creation of a strategic implementation plan, identifying product/process priorities and key goals. Top management must support the company-wide *world-class* strategy and become familiar with the *world-class* concepts and technologies. A commitment from top management must be obtained, and their involvement is strongly encouraged. Lack of commitment or wishy-washy commitments are danger signals. An implementation organization is then formed with clearly stated objectives, responsibilities and time frames. Demand Flow manufacturing implementations should not become career jobs. Positive results should be visible in a targeted time frame. Any plant taking more than a year to implement Demand Flow manufacturing may be mired in a "perpetual implementation"—a term familiar to MRP II practitioners.

Educating on One Track

An education plan must also be developed. Top management, the implementation team and other key personnel must receive consistent, detailed Demand Flow manufacturing education. There are many brands of lead time reduction and inventory reduction, but there is only one technology of *world-class* Demand Flow manufacturing, and all employees must share the same technology. Varying approaches will swiftly derail the implementation. The deeper the education process can be driven into an organization, the higher the chances for success within the planned time frame.

Follow Steps; Make Determinations

The next step is to start the development of the Demand Flow production process. This starts by establishing a TQC sequence of events and a product synchronization chart for each process. This natural flow of the product will identify work content, TQC points and nonvalue-added steps. Then, based upon the highest desired manufacturing rate, a targeted operational cycle time for a process is determined. Operational method sheets, which clearly show the work content at each operation, TQC and verification data, are then generated. Bills of material are compressed into piles of parts with their associated backflush locations. If necessary, intermediate deduct points are also identified. Mixed-model lines and cells are determined from process mapping and group technology techniques. Total product cycle time is calculated and will become the basis for inventory investment and the application of overhead. Initial line designs are now sketched out—on paper only!

Marketing Key in Flexibility

In the next stage, negotiations occur with marketing to determine the limits of flexibility required to compete and support the customers. Marketing establishes the forecast, outlines flexibility windows, and owns the responsibility of finished goods. Also in this stage, TQC and employee involvement programs begin. All employees will be trained on simple, statistical problem-solving techniques. Employee involvement teams will be formed with training provided on the employee involvement projects and group dynamics. A responsive and flexible pay and reward mechanism should be developed at this point as well. A training program to certify a minimum of one-up and one-down employee flexibility within the process also is established at this point.

Procurement will also begin discussions with suppliers during this stage. They will inform the suppliers, via a Supplier Day, that, while Demand Flow manufacturing has not yet been fully implemented, it is a strategic goal of the company. The company eventually will be working more closely with a smaller number of suppliers and much greater emphasis on flexibility and quality will be required. Kanban pull strategies that require supplier participation will also be explained.

Plan, Design and Do It

Based upon the earlier line design, the next stage will include calculating in-process and RIP material Kanbans for each operation. Once this is completed, the physical change of the line layout and converting the back portion of the product to the Demand Flow process can proceed. Once the Demand Flow process achieves 90-95 percent linearity, the pull process can expand to include supplier pulls. Transportation networks will be established; DFT supplier contracts will be negotiated for class "A" parts for the target line; and RIP areas and pull sequences will be established.

At this time, the Kanban and inventory management will include the backflush technique based upon the Demand Flow manufacturing "pile of parts" bill of material. Also, testing of the costing system to a total product cycle time basis and completing the modification of compensation and organizational systems is now completed.

Management reports are produced at the end of the day to ensure the daily rates are achieved in a productive and flexible flow process. Minor changes in Kanban sizing and method sheet management should also be expected. Minor modification to the previously tested formal system should also be expected. Demand Flow lines that are properly designed should become linear within three working days of physical line change.

When this implementation is followed and completed, the *world-class* Demand Flow manufacturer will have a very simple, yet powerful, manufacturing weapon and can now compete with anyone in the world.

Dust, Survival or Leadership

The world is changing. Results and techniques that worked in the past will not be "good enough" in the future. Traditional manufacturers will never evolve into *world-class* competitors. Tomorrow's leaders will be born by visionary corporate leaders who desire results that are a *Quantum Leap* beyond those achieved by the techniques, methods, and systems currently in place today. The *world-class winners* will apply the *speed-to-market* and Demand Flow Technology to prominent positions of market leadership. The traditional *losers* will convince themselves that they are unique and that Demand Flow manufacturing won't work in "their" industry, no matter what industry they are temporarily in at this time.

Taking the Right Turn

Western manufacturing is at a crossroads. In one direction, there is the continuation of the death spiral toward a service-based economy with the inevitable decline in the standard of living for future generations. The other direction holds a renewed commitment by individuals and companies to be the best in the world. To be the best is to be leaders in the *speed-to-market* implementation of technology—to produce the highest quality products at the lowest possible cost and to use manufacturing as a profit generating competitive weapon.

The road to be the best, however, will not be a path of gentle evolution. Leaders with vision must abandon the outdated manufacturing techniques of yesterday. They must break the mindsets of today, grasp the Demand Flow Technology of tomorrow, and make the *Quantum Leap* to *world-class* excellence.

Glossary

ACQUISITION COST

The costs associated with buying purchased material. Usually expressed as a percentage adder to the purchased material standard cost. Acquisition costs include procurement, shipping and inspection costs.

ATP

Available to Promise (ATP). The quantity of a product that is available for sales to promise to customers. ATP exists when the total demand is greater than actual orders.

BACKFLUSH

The method in Demand Flow manufacturing of relieving RIP inventory of a product's bill of material quantities/usage when that product is completed at the end of the flow process. May also be used to relieve purchase orders for consigned inventory material.

BATCH MANUFACTURING

The traditional manufacturing philosophy of producing a product in scheduled lots or quantities. Usually includes work orders that are created per a schedule for a quantity of fabricated parts or subassemblies. This often causes material to be issued from a store's location based upon the predetermined schedule.

BILL OF MATERIAL

The listing of material used to make a product, usually multilevel in traditional manufacturing; usually single-level in a Demand Flow manufacturing company.

CAPACITY

The highest targeted volume output of products that is planned to be achieved by a Demand Flow manufacturing process. This is the management-defined quantity that the Demand Flow process must be designed to support, usually stated in products per day (Dcp).

CELL

A cell is a grouping of dissimilar resources (people and/or machines) in a logical and sequential manner to facilitate the flow of a product or products. Cells are typically scheduled in traditional manufacturing and they are pulled using Kanban in a Demand Flow manufacturing environment. See Group Technology.

DAILY RATE

The rolling daily production plan. This rate is determined each day based upon the number of shippable products completed at the end of the production process. The daily rate is adjusted each day based upon the actual customer demand.

DEMAND-BASED PLANNING

A production and purchased material planning methodology utilized in Demand Flow Technology. Demand time fences, planning flex fences and Total Demand calculations are tools uniquely applicable to this methodology. Through the use of flex fences, supplier requirements are independent of anticipated production plans.

DEMAND TIME FENCE

The future planning time fence where total demand is independent of forecast and must be driven by customer demand. Total demand cannot be changed within this time fence.

DUAL CARD KANBAN

A demand pull technique that uses a "move" and "produce" communication method. It is typically used in machine-intensive manufacturing processes or independent cells where setups or long replenishment times are present.

FEEDER PROCESS

A branch process that feeds directly into a consuming operation or flow process. The feeder is always identified independently of the consuming process on the product synchronization. (See Product Synchronization).

FLOW RATE

The current daily rate divided by effective work hours in a shift multiplied by the number of shifts in a day. An important volume-related management criteria that should be adjusted daily, based upon current customer demand.

ERP

Enterprise Requirements Planning - MRP II (by another name) with the addition of electronic communication to Computer Aided Design (CAD), Computer Aided

Manufacturing (CAM), Electronic Office Communications and other financial and distribution systems.

FORECAST CONSUMPTION

A technique which is used to determine the production plan, first with a blend of forecast and sales orders, then on actual orders alone. A Demand-Based planning tool used to coordinate marketing, production and outside suppliers.

FRU

A Field Replaceable Unit, or spare. In Demand Flow Technology, a FRU is treated as an independent product. The FRU is an independent product that is forecast, manufactured and costed independently of any other product. It is typically produced in a mixed-model line with other complete products.

GROUP TECHNOLOGY

The technology of organizing people and different functional machines into cells to produce related parts or products. The focus of the cell is to reduce inventory, reduce or eliminate queues, improve quality and reduce throughput times.

HOMOGENEOUS OVERHEAD

A financial pool of fixed or variable overhead costs that is required to convert material into a finished product. Homogeneous overhead cost pools are typically applicable to all products being produced.

IN-PROCESS KANBAN

An inventory of component material or in-process inventory that is required to support designed imbalances between DFT operations. An in-process Kanban never has "part number" identity and is usually represented by the letter "X" painted on the card, table or floor.

INTERMEDIATE BACKFLUSH

An inventory transaction that is performed to relieve RIP inventory that is consumed into a product up to a physical location in the manufacturing line. Material relieved from RIP is considered to be in a "holding" in-process bucket which will later be relieved through either an end of the line backflush transaction or a scrap transaction. An intermediate backflush can be used as a physical point for scrap transactions but can also be used for process audit inventory purposes.

INTERMEDIATE DEDUCT ID

A physical location in a Demand Flow line at which an intermediate backflush occurs.

INVENTORY CARRYING COSTS

The actual costs associated with maintaining inventory in a company. These costs apply to raw, RIP and finished goods inventory. Typically between 25 and 40 percent of the value of inventory is generally accepted as the cost of holding/carrying that inventory. May include the cost of money, the cost of inventory storage, inventory management, scrap and obsolescence, taxes and lost opportunity costs.

INVENTORY TURNS

The number of times inventory turns over in one year. Calculation: Annual estimated inventory requirements divided by current total on-hand inventory.

J-I-T

Just-In-Time. A western culture term often associated with a manufacturing technique which is based on a flow and pull manufacturing process rather than traditional scheduling techniques. It is often misunderstood as a Just-In-Time inventory reduction program by western philosophers and observers. The J-I-T technique is only a very small piece in the Demand Flow Technology.

KANBAN

The Japanese word which defines a communication signal or card. It is the technique that is used to pull products and material through and into the Demand Flow manufacturing process. It can be a physical signal such as a container or card. Information on a raw material Kanban identifies part number and description information plus points of usage/consumption and supply/replenishment along with a calculated quantity.

LABOR HOURS

The required time to complete manufacturing steps by people in order for a product to meet design or production specifications.

LINEARITY

Monitored at the back of the production flow (completion), it is the relationship of planned daily rates versus actual production. A primary Demand Flow manufacturing objective: to adjust the volume and mix of products every day based upon actual customer demand and to meet the planned daily rate every day.

MACHINE CELL

A machine cell is a grouping of dissimilar machines in a logical and sequential manner to facilitate the flow of a product or products. Machine cells are typically scheduled in traditional manufacturing and they are pulled using Kanban in a Demand Flow manufacturing environment. See Group Technology.

MACHINE TIME

The required time to complete manufacturing steps performed by machines in order for products to meet design or product specifications.

MIXED-MODEL DEMAND FLOW LINE

A primary goal of Demand Flow manufacturing is to design flow lines to produce families of similar products. The Mixed-Model Demand Flow line has the ability to build a range of volumes of any product, any day, based upon the direction of actual customer demand. Quality is designed into the line and executed through TQC operational method sheets.

MIXED-MODEL SEQUENCING

Sequencing is the serial order in which the total demand of products and options is to be pulled into a mixed-model Demand Flow line. Sequencing products is also a balancing technique used to minimize imbalances between products to be produced in the same mixed-model Demand Flow line.

MOVE TIME

Time spent in moving products or materials from one point to another, either with people or machines. Appreciable move time usually indicates a poorly designed line.

MRP

Material Requirements Planning. The outdated computerized scheduling system. Used to schedule material requirements from suppliers as well as internal production.

MRP II

Manufacturing Resource Planning. Another later version of MRP that is also an outdated computer scheduling system. Similar to MRP, plus these systems have additional complexity to track production through work centers and departments.

NONREPLENISHABLE KANBAN

A type of material Kanban that is not replenished when emptied. This type of Kanban must be managed and will typically be used for custom products, one-time customer orders, or for very infrequent material demands.

NONVALUE-ADDED

Steps in the production process that may currently be necessary but do not increase the worth of a product or service to a customer.

OPERATION

A grouping of tasks (work elements) from a Sequence of Events that defines work to be performed. This grouping of tasks, based on their accumulated times, is intended to be equal to or less than the Operational Cycle Time target. An operation in DFT is where work is performed by a person or a machine.

OPERATIONAL CYCLE TIME

The calculated target of work content time to be performed independently by a person or machine in a Demand Flow line. It is calculated by multiplying the effective work hours times the number of shifts and dividing the result by the designed capacity of products to be produced in the Demand Flow line. Design capacity is per product and it is determined by management and marketing projections.

OPERATIONAL TQC METHOD SHEETS

This is always a "colored" graphic representation of quality criteria and work content as defined by the sequence of events. Graphically illustrated sheets with little or no text that communicate to production employees, simply and clearly, what the work content is at the operation, what to verify and where to look to ensure Total Quality of previous operational work.

PARETO

Pareto is the act of tracking the occurences and frequency of opportunities for improvement at every operation in a process.

PARTICIPATORY MANAGEMENT

A departure from traditional departmental management and a move toward team management. Includes membership from multiple disciplines such as marketing, engineering, production, quality, materials, etc.

PILE OF PARTS

Individual components or parts required to manufacture a product. These parts are not structured in a traditional multilevel, subassembly or fabricated part method. This becomes a flat listing of purchased parts required to build a product.

PLANNING FLEX FENCE

Negotiated flexibility time frame outside the demand fence. The total demand and the resulting planned daily rate can be varied within predetermined product parameters that are based on flexibility requirements negotiated with marketing/customers. Material requirements are negotiated with suppliers mirroring the flexibility provided to marketing/customers.

PLANNING VISIBILITY

The long-range forecast for requirements which is used both internally and with suppliers for planning purposes. Forecasted requirements with flex windows information is shared with all "pull" suppliers.

PROCESS

A DFT grouping of logical and functional manufacturing steps that are to be performed to convert material

toward becoming a completed product. Work performed in a process will be defined as a Sequence of
Events.

PROCESS MAPPING

A matrix of processes defined by the product synchronizations. A Demand Flow technique used to determine
the commonality of manufacturing processes and commonality of products. The objective of process mapping
is to develop families of products that share common
processes to see which products can be produced in the
same mixed-model Demand Flow line.

PRODUCT SYNCHRONIZATION

A design engineering technique used in the implementation of the Demand Flow Business Strategy to define
the relationships of manufacturing processes to produce
a product. A product synchronization defines the phased
relationship of all manufacturing processes required to
build a product. It will be used as a basis for the design
of the product as well as the design for the Demand Flow
line.

PULL SEQUENCES

A chain of information identifying points of usage/con-
sumption and supply/replenishment, which will form

the path along which Kanban material is replenished through the Demand Flow manufacturing process. Pull sequences are "from" and "to" relationships that tie into Kanban replenishment time frames for Kanban sizing.

QUEUE

Waiting time or inventory buildup in the traditional batch or scheduling manufacturing environment. Queue or wait time never appears in a TQC sequence of events and is never part of operational definition.

QUICK COUNT

A methodology to replenish material Kanbans that uses approximate replenishment quantities (e.g., handful, fill, cupful, pallet). This method is always used within RIP when no special need to count the material precisely exists.

RIP

An inventory management term used in Demand Flow manufacturing, Raw-In-Process inventory. Excluding the material in the storeroom, this includes all raw and in-process materials that are at supply points in or close to the production line and feeder processes. RIP is supplied by the storeroom and/or directly by suppliers. Material quantities pulled into RIP are acknowledged

by quantity when entering; material and production
movements from any point to another within RIP are
not counted or tracked. Once the product is complete
and leaves production, the Bill of Material listing of
component parts is relieved from RIP inventory by a
backflush transaction. The only other counting and
tracking within RIP is for scraped material.

SCRAP

Unusable parts or materials treated the same in Demand
Flow manufacturing as in traditional manufacturing—
always reported as scrap occurs.

SEQUENCE OF EVENTS

Defines the required work and quality criteria to build
a product in a specific production process. This is never
the anticipated work content, independent of the production environment, methods, specific machine types
or quality criteria. Contains the natural sequence of
events required to produce a product to its product and
process design specification. Identifies sequential work
content and specific TQC information against each task.
It is one of the essential techniques of the Demand Flow
Technology. Drives operational definition and is the
basis for all work, line design, mixed-model planning
and TQC method sheet design.

SETUP TIME

Nonvalue-added steps/work that are necessary prior to being able to add value to a part or product. Can range from unwrapping parts to making tooling adjustments on a large machine.

SINGLE-SOURCE SUPPLIER

A supplier that was specifically selected over other qualified suppliers to receive all of the expected business on a particular part or component.

SOCIO-PRODUCTION

The extreme experiment in liberal management philosophy. Now in use by very few companies, it provides employees with great hiring, decision-making and leadership latitude in impacting company operations. Although excellent in philosophical concept and theory, it tends to draw out the decision-making process and reduces the speed in which new products could be introduced.

SOLE-SOURCE SUPPLIER

A supplier who is the only known supplier of a particular material or component. Manufacturers that require the specific part or material sold by this supplier can only purchase this item from this supplier.

SUBASSEMBLIES

Components that are assembled or processed together to meet a specific design drawing or function. This portion of the product has its own part number and bill of material and it is later used in the final construction of a finished product.

TAKT TIME

A word with heritage from the German language that translates into English as rhythm or beat (a musical term). In Demand Flow Technology it defines the targeted work content for people and machines to meet the production capacity that the Demand Flow line was designed to achieve. Each process on the dedicated product synchronization or mixed-model process map may have a different Takt time if they have a different volume or yield. Mathematically always defined by the operational cycle time calculation.

TEAM PASS

The tagging or flagging of a portion of a manufactured product that has been found to be defective because of faulty workmanship. A team pass product has passed

Index

A

Acquisition cost: 275
    definition: 323
Available to promise (ATP): 88
    definition: 323

B

Backflush: 106 - 107, 121 - 123, 300
    definition: 323
    Intermediate: 125, 300
    Intermediate, definition: 328
Batch manufacturing: 24
    definition: 324
Bill of material (BOM): 121, 124, 155, 159, 161 - 162, 169 - 171,
    299
    definition: 324
    Planning: 175
Buyer: 211

C

Capacity: 47
    definition: 324
Cell: 26, 138
    definition: 324
Certification: 239 - 242
Checklists: 142, 144
Commitment: 316
Compensation: 227, 230 - 232
Computer: 7, 17, 92, 104, 289, 291, 293, 295, 297, 299, 301,
    303, 305, 307, 309
    Network: 308
Continual improvement: 262
Control chart: 83
Cpk: 256 - 258

D

Daily rate: 27, 49, 71, 82, 100, 234
    definition: 325
Demand Flow
    Manufacturing: 18, 27, 30, 70, 76
    Technology: 8, 24
Demand time fence: 70, 73, 84, 86, 89
    definition: 325
Demand-Based planning: 75, 78, 80 - 81, 83, 298, 303
    definition: 325

through two operations where defective work was performed but incorrectly verified and improperly validated to a TQC specification. A team pass product will not be credited in the analysis of the daily linearity index.

TOTAL DEMAND

Total demand is the projected, and eventually the planned, quantity of products that are to be produced. Based upon the marketing flex windows this is independent of the demand for purchased material. Outside the demand planning fence, Total Demand is determined by taking the greater of forecast or actual orders. Within the demand time fence it is the actual customer demand that has been smoothed, and this demand will become the daily rate at the back of the production line.

TOTAL PRODUCT CYCLE TIME

Starting from the completion of the product (FGI), the accumulated work content time along the longest path of the product synchronization (TP c/t). Typically less than the total work content hours to build a product. Can only equal the total time to build a product in a simple product with feeder processes or concurrent work. The time inventory is required to support the processes to build a product.

TQC

The Total Quality Control technique in Demand Flow manufacturing which brings quality into the manufacturing process at the point where work is being performed. TQC is defined by the sequence of events and it occurs at every step in the production process, as compared with external inspection points found in traditional manufacturing environments.

VALUE-ADDED

Steps in the production process that increase the worth of a product or service to an external customer or consumer. The part of the product and process specification the customer is expecting and willing to pay to receive.

WORK CONTENT

The required work that is performed to build a product to its specification. Includes setup, move, nonvalue, value-added and quality work.

N

Nonvalue-added: 24, 41 - 42, 46, 61, 141
   definition: 333

O

One-up, one-down: 133, 157, 228, 233
Operation: 50, 52, 54, 59, 180
   definition: 333
Operational cycle time (OP c/t):   33, 36, 47, 49, 53 - 55, 58 - 59,
   138
   definition: 333
Options: 176
Organization: 312 - 313
Overhead: 66
   Flow-based: 270
   Homogeneous: 271 - 272
   Homogeneous, definition: 328

P

Packaging strategy: 205
Pareto: 260
   definition: 334
Participatory management
   definition: 334
Pay for skill: 230 - 232
Pay program: 231 - 244
Pile of parts: 155, 160, 162
   definition: 335

Q

R